Kid
CULTURE

The Hip Parent's Handbook to
Navigating Books, Music, T.V.,
and Movies in the Digital Age

By Todd Tobias and Lou Harry

CIDER MILL
PRESS

BOOK
PUBLISHERS

Kennebunkport, Maine

13-Digit ISBN: 978-1-60433-025-0
10-Digit ISBN: 1-60433-025-2

This book may be ordered by mail from the publisher.
Please include $2.50 for postage and handling.
Please support your local bookseller first!

Books published by Cider Mill Press Book Publishers are available at special discounts for bulk purchases in the United States by corporations, institutions, and other organizations. For more information, please contact the publisher.

Cider Mill Press Book Publishers
"Where good books are ready for press"
12 Port Farm Road
Kennebunkport, Maine 04046

Visit us on the Web!
WWW.CIDERMILLPRESS.COM

Design by Alicia Freile
Typography: Bodega Sans, Concorde, Univers, and Zapf Dingbats

Cover Images Copyright: Selcuk Acar, Pawel Strykowski, Konstantin Tavrov, Jonphoto, and Greenland, 2008
All used under license from Shutterstock.com

Printed in China

1 2 3 4 5 6 7 8 9 0
First Edition

Todd: For my sister, Paige Button, one of the greatest parents in the history of parenting. And for *Family Ties'* Steven Keaton, my all-time favorite pop-culture parent. Sit, Ubu, sit! Good dog!

✳ ✳ ✳

Lou: For my brother, George, another one of the greatest parents in the history of parenting. And for *It's a Wonderful Life's* George Bailey, my all-time favorite pop-culture parent. Ha, ha, ha, ha! My mouth's bleeding, Bert! My mouth's bleeding! Zuzu's petals . . . Zuzu . . .

Contents

INTRODUCTION..8

PART. I: BOOKS..10

Classics Caution...12

Seven Bookshelf Musts 16

I'm Board: How Can Something with So Few Words Be So Good? 20

A Special Tribute to *Goodnight Moon*...21

Where the Wild Things Are: So Good, It's Scary 24

A Special Dissing of *The Tale of Peter Rabbit*......................................27

Wait, You Didn't Say This Book Was Going to Be on the Test 28

The Worstiest Worst of Dr. Seuss 30

The Grover Library...32

25 Reasons Why Celebrities Should Not Write Children's Books

    (and Why You Should Avoid Them) 33

A Few Celebrity-Authored Books That Are Actually Quite Good 36

The Search is On: Hunting for Waldo et. al. 41

Noisy Books: "The Cow Says…Moo." The Parent Says,

"Throw This Damn Thing Against the Wall." 42

Too Hip for the Pre-School: Postmodern Kid Books 43

Enough Already: Disposable Kid Books..46

Books Based on Movie/TV Shows and Why to Avoid Them.........................48

Ten Books to Know That We Couldn't Fit In Anywhere Else........................49

Intermezzo: **The Wonderful Evolution of Oz** 52

PART II: TV AND VIDEO

PART II: TV AND VIDEO 58

12 Moments Where the Muppets are as Great as Anything Ever

Created by Mankind..60

The ABCs of Kiddie TV: An Abridged Encyclopedia....................................62

Sesame Test: This Quiz Has Been Brought to You By the Letter *Q*............71

Barney and Friends vs. *Bear in the Big Blue House*

(With an Assist from *The Teletubbies*) 74

Superhero Substitutions 77

God is in the Tomato 81

A Host of Changes (or, Wait, What Happened to the Other Guy?)..............83

Ten Children's TV Shows to Know That We Couldn't Fit In Anywhere Else 87

Intermezzo: **Oh the Places Dr. Seuss Has Gone**...91

PART III: MUSIC 96

Why It's Okay for You to Hate Children's Entertainers 98

The Six Classes of Kids' Musicians...99

Our Favorite Performances of Children's Songs by Famous Entertainers 100

Great Adult Songs that Could Easily Be Passed Off As Children's Songs................105

Music Quiz: The Songs Remain the Same...106

But Isn't It Really About, *You* Know, Drugs?

    The Definitive Dope on "Puff the Magic Dragon".......................................108

A Wiggly Primer for the Uninitiated Parent...110

How to Tell the Beatles from the Wiggles 114

When *You* Need a Good Cry 116

Why *Schoolhouse Rock* Still Rocks 117

Ten Songs To Know That We Couldn't Fit in Anywhere Else................................120

Intermezzo: The Ever-Changing, Always-Constant World of Charlie Brown 121

PART IV: MOVIES 126

What's in a Rating? 128

The Disney Animated Feature Canon Part 1: The Walt Years...............................130

The Disney Princesses Quiz 144

The Disney Animated Feature Canon Part 2: The Post-Walt Years........................148

Disney Live Action to Watch/Avoid 165

You've Got Animation in My Live Action/You've Got Live Action

   in My Animation 170

Pixar Sticks 172

Hey, What's He/She Doing in a Kid Flick? 173

The Other Guys: The Best of Non-Disney Traditional Animation Feature Films 174

Ten Movies to Know That We Couldn't Fit in Anywhere Else 176

PART V: CHARACTERS, CHARACTERS EVERYWHERE 178

Theater: *Annie,* et al. 180

Arena Shows: Better Skate Then Never 183

Chance Encounters: Board Games, Your Kid, and You 184

Breakfast Cereal: Your Sugar-pushing Friends 185

Live: Look Honey, It's the Real Mickey! 186

AFTERWORD 188
QUIZ ANSWERS 189
INDEX 194
ABOUT THE AUTHORS 203

Introduction

The Wiggles. Elmo. Bob the Builder. The Pirates Who Don't Do Anything. Horton. Simba. Walter the Farting Dog. Dora and Diego. Charlie Brown and Lucy. Eubie, Wayne, Twinkle, and Kip. Little Bill. Lilo. Ariel and Belle. Lolly and his adverbs. Farkle McBride. The Man in the Yellow Hat. Pinky Dinky Doo. Mulan and the rest of the Disney Princesses, The Pokey Little Puppy . . . .

A kid toddling around the world today has a whole bunch of interesting friends, and as a parent, shouldn't you get to know them?

That's what *Kid Culture* is all about.

In the pages that follow, we'll take you on a guided tour through the often overwhelming world of kid culture. We'll start in the book stacks, click through TV and video, turn up the music, and go to the movies again and again. We hope the trip will be enlightening, entertaining, and ultimately useful in helping both you and your child.

Are we advocating excessive media exposure for your kid? Of course not. In fact, we agree with the American Academy of Pediatrics, which advises that no children under two should watch *any* TV for the first few years.

Just because we agree with it, though, doesn't mean we've lived by it. (FYI, co-author Lou is the father of four kids, co-author Todd has two.) But if you can go TV-free, more power to you.

For the rest of us, let's be practical. Show me a parent with a TV in the house who hasn't parked his kid there when the phone rings, when there's food on the stove, or when the spouse has a meeting run late, and I'll show you a liar. Why else does *Teletubbies* exist?

Our philosophy is simple: no matter what your degree of entertainment consumption, knowledge is a good thing. And since we never had a guide book when our respective first children appeared, we thought it was time to write one. Shouldn't every parent have a handy guide to this complex and ever-growing universe of child entertainment?

At this point, we could get all academic on you. But we understand that this parenting thing is a more than full-time gig, and we're amazed that you've even had time to pick up this book at all. So we're not going to waste your time here or in the chapters to come. Feel free to skip around, browse, or read it in one-paragraph incre-ments. No pressure on you, you've got a lot on your hands.

So let's get right to it.

Part I

BOOKS

In the beginning, it is said, was the word. And that's good enough for us. We're big on children's books, believing wholeheartedly that reading to a kid early and often not only ups the little one's curiosity and speeds along a thirst for knowledge, it also feels great for both child and parent.

Ideally, the book is so good that when that little head gets heavy and the eyes close, you still want to continue reading. It won't happen all the time, but when it does, it's magic. That's because the creators of children's books can be as good at what they do as the creators of any other form of literature. Just try to imagine a world without Horton or the Tin Woodsman.

Now, come back to the real world. There's a lot to sort through when building a library of kid lit. We're here to help. Read on.

Classics Caution

any new parents find themselves wanting to do everything right. No molded plastic toys for their kids; it's wooden blocks. Battery operated trains? Where's the imagination in that? And don't even get these parents started on the Disney versions of classic stories. For their story times, it's the original tales or nothing.

Well, you might want to think again before you join this elite crew—especially on that last note.

Because while Disney certainly has, well, Disney-fied the classics, in the process they've also helped make them palatable, especially for the youngest kids. Still think you want to expose them to the originals? Here are introductions to the three classics, which today would garner PG-13s at best.

CINDERELLA

A hard-knock life for an ill-treated stepdaughter is transformed by a magical evening at a ball, thanks to a magical fairy godmother, a glass slipper, and a handsome prince. What could be more palatable?

Well, as you'll see, the Grimm Brothers didn't just have that name because of their family of origin. The original version of *Cinderella*, without a fairy godmother in sight, includes such great moments as the Prince smearing the steps with pitch to catch Cinderella, who has already run away two other times (once including a narrow escape by way of a pear tree).

Cindy's unexplainable runaway-bride-to-be flight mechanism isn't the problematic part. No, for that, you have to wait until it's time to try on the famed shoe (gold here, not glass). Here, the stepsisters show their true desperation by, in turn, cutting off a toe and a heel–of their feet–in order to make the damn thing fit. Graphic enough for you? Well, in both cases, the Prince doesn't notice until he's got his potential brides on horseback and sees the blood spilling out from the shoe.

Oh, and guess what happens when the stepsisters show up to the wedding? Cinderella's pigeon friends pluck their eyes out. End of story. Now, sleep tight, darling.

PINOCCHIO

Remember the cute Disney kid who occasionally strayed a bit from the straight and narrow but inside his wooden body had a good heart? Well, you might not recognize him in Carlo Collodi's *The Adventures of Pinocchio*.

The bratty kid sticks out his tongue at Geppetto as soon as he has a mouth, pulls off the guy's wig as soon as he has fingers, and kicks him as soon as he has legs. (Maybe it's hereditary: Even before the kid enters the scene, Geppetto–described as a guy with a very bad temper–gets into a scratching and biting fight with the carpenter, who discovered the odd piece of talking wood.)

You might assume that Jiminy Cricket would be there to help guide the wayward lad. You'd be wrong. An advice-dispensing cricket does show up in chapter 4– Pinocchio delivers a blow to the head of the insect. Writes Collodi: "With a last weak 'cri-cri-ci' the poor Cricket fell from the wall, dead!" (He does briefly return later as a ghost.)

After that, you might not be surprised to find that Pinocchio gets hung at the end of chapter 15, which was life-of-the-party Collodi's original ending for the story.

But at the request of his no-doubt flabbergasted publisher, he went back to the inkwell and wrote another twenty chapters, allowing the pine kid to be redeemed . . . but not until spending four months in prison, crying over the grave of the Blue Fairy (here called the Lovely Maiden with Azure Hair) and facing accusations of killing a fellow student with a school book.

Read this to your kids? Wood you? We wood-nt.

THE LITTLE MERMAID

Wish you could be part of her world? Better think again.

In the Hans Christian Anderson original, not only is it the sisters of this nameless girl who are interested in the stuff found in sunken ships, they also are in the habit of singing on the surface and inadvertently luring sailors to their deaths. When the little mermaid (not named Ariel, by the way—nobody here has a name) finally does rise to the surface, it is with eight giant oysters painfully attached to her tail at the insistence, for no clear reason, of her grandmother.

While she does rescue a prince from drowning, they don't make eye contact right away. Instead, she turns into a kind of sea-stalker, tracking him to his castle and obsessing over him from a distance.

This is when we get a major fact omitted from most future versions: merpeople don't have immortal souls. They may have a three-hundred-year lifespan, but once they are gone, sorry, no eternal life. So when the little mermaid considers opting in to this whole human-with-legs thing, it's not strictly for love.

"I would give gladly all the hundreds of years that I have to live," she says, "to be a human being only for one day, and to have the hope of knowing the happiness of that glorious world above the stars." If she gets a dude to love her—and commit in front of a priest—then she'll get a soul.

The sea witch is there, but in addition to being scary, she's also got the crushed skeletons of every lost sailor—and animal—in her grasp. " . . . even a little mermaid, whom they had caught and strangled." Her home, of course, is also made of bones. Waste not, want not.

The legs the sea witch is offering come with a few catches. In addition to losing her voice, " . . . at every step you take it will feel as if you were treading upon sharp knives," and, "The first morning after he marries another, your heart will break, and you will become foam on the crest of the waves."

Sound like bad stuff's a comin'? Just you wait. The Prince loves her—as a child. He falls hard for a neighboring princess and marries her. Adding insult to injury, the little mermaid has to be the one carrying the princess bride's train as she marries the prince. On the wedding night, the mermaid's sisters explain that they cut off their hair and gave it to the witch in exchange for a knife. With that knife, the little mermaid is to kill the prince, let the blood fall on her feet, and voila, she'll have a tail again.

She doesn't go through with it, although she does go through a transformation. Turns out grandma was wrong. She can get an immortal soul, although she has to wait three hundred years as a dead soulless spirit for it.

The coda, though, may be the most disturbing part of the story. It's a warning to kids: every time a kid is naughty, the dead mermaids cry, and for every tear they shed, a day is added to their wait for heaven.

Call us middlebrow, but we kind of prefer Ariel marrying Prince Eric.

Seven Bookshelf Musts

Okay, so if you skip those classics, what *should* be on every kid's bookshelf? There's lots of great kid lit out there, including these must-haves:

THE VELVETEEN RABBIT

In this enduring story, a stuffed toy rabbit learns what it means to be "real." The answer? Being loved and loving in return. When the titular hero is given as a Christmas present to a young boy, the toy rabbit begins to wonder about the nature of identity. He befriends a tattered Skin Horse—one of the oldest and wisest toys in the nursery—who reveals the goal of all of the resident playthings: to be made real through the love of their owner. "Real isn't how you are made," said the Skin Horse. "It's a thing that happens to you. When a child loves you for a long, long time, not just to play with, but really loves you, then you become Real." Margery Williams's eloquent tale of a tail has been engaging readers since it was first published in 1922.

Sentimental and heartfelt, the story will move parents and children alike.

THE ADVENTURES OF HAROLD AND THE PURPLE CRAYON

Crockett Johnson's tribute to the imagination and the places it can take you is as fresh and, well, colorful today as it was when it was first published in 1955. This timeless tale chronicles the adventures of Harold, a cherubic young lad whose oversized purple crayon lends him the power to create different worlds. Each adventure blends into the next, and Harold must quickly think on his feet to save himself from his own creations. When he draws an apple tree, for example, he soon realizes he needs to draw a dragon to protect it (duh!). But the dragon is a tad too frightening and causes our little hero's hand to shake. So an ocean is inadvertently created. What's Harold to do? Draw a boat, of course. Then sail on through a variety of other challenges he and his trusty crayon must confront. This gentle story teaches kids that even the best laid plans go awry, but by keeping your wits about you, anything is possible out in the big wide world.

MADELINE

Of all the twelve little Parisian girls under the supervision of a nun named Miss Clavel, Madeline is not just the smallest—she's also the bravest. Mice or winter don't faze her. And "to the tiger in the zoo Madeline just said pooh-pooh." *Madeline*, the first of a series of books (and later a TV series and feature film) by Ludwig Bemelmans, introduces us to a character who has become one of the most memorable heroines in all of children's literature. Each book in the series shows Madeline's courage and kindness in the face of adversity. In this first series installment, even an emergency appendectomy can't dampen the plucky little one's spirits. With easy-to-read prose and attractive illustrations by the author himself, Madeline is not just a positive role model (for young girls especially), she's the star of a book you'll be reading at many bedtimes to come.

THE POKEY LITTLE PUPPY

A group of puppy siblings routinely enjoy heading out into the "wide, wide world" to see what adventures can be found. But one pokey little puppy always dawdles behind because he has a knack for sniffing out his mother's yummy desserts. While his brothers are always denied these treats as punishment for leaving the yard, the Pokey Little Puppy—who always brings up the rear—manages to avoid reprimand.

For a while, anyway. First published in 1942 as part of Simon and Schuster's first Little Golden Book series, Janette Sebring Lowrey's story about a pup with little pep remains one of the best-selling hardcover children's books of all-time. Eventually, the pokey one's dawdling ways catch up with him. The book concludes with him returning home too late to enjoy his mother's strawberry shortcake, of which his brothers have made short work. The titular pup goes to bed with an empty stomach and feeling "very sorry for himself." The moral? Snap to it, kid! A quick, easy read, *The Pokey Little Puppy* has been entertaining generations of children and you'll enjoy introducing it to yours.

THE LITTLE ENGINE THAT COULD

Never underestimate the value of a positive mental attitude is the theme of this good old children's standby. When a train full of toys breaks down, it's up to a small switching engine to lead the train over a mountain so that the toys can be delivered to the children on the other side. But since the little train has never been over the mountain, pulling the heavy load seems like a daunting task. What to do? Think positively. "I think I can, I think I can, I think I can," repeats that little engine over and over again. And sure enough, all that positivity pays off in the end.

CURIOUS GEORGE

For children, curiosity often leads to mischief. Same goes for monkeys—especially ones named George. In H. A. Rey's *Curious George,* first published in 1941, we're introduced to the sassy simian who has become the star of a series of books, a TV show, and a major motion picture—not to mention becoming something of a household name. In this book, The Man in the Yellow Hat finds George (some cynics say he kidnaps George) in the jungle and brings him back home with the idea of donating him to a zoo. But before that can happen, things get curiouser and curiouser with George jumping into the ocean, calling the fire department, landing in (and escaping from) jail, and stealing some high-flying balloons.

But it all works out in the end. And in the process, children are taught that there are consequences for every decision curious little minds have a way of making.

PAT THE BUNNY

First published in 1940, *Pat the Bunny* is not the name of a character. Rather, it's a call to action for small children. Interactive "touch and feel" activities found in this, one of the best-selling children's books of all time, include playing peek-a-boo, smelling flowers, looking in the mirror, feeling a dad's scratchy face, and trying on a ring. Written by Dorothy Kunhardt, this quick read's playful encouragement of sensory activities will keep your child engaged for a good five whole minutes! Which is better than nothing.

I'm Board: How Can Something with So Few Words Be So Good?

oard books are different than other kinds of books. For starters, the pages and covers are made out of cardboard. Hence, board books.

Sometimes when you ask your child if she would like you to read her a board book, in your mind you are really pronouncing it "bored book." That's because board books use spare, simple language. This is not *always* a bad thing.

GUESS HOW MUCH I LOVE YOU. FREIGHT TRAIN. RUNAWAY BUNNY

These books are quick, easy reads. These books are classics. You should consider adding them to your collection. You'll read them over and over again.

Other bored books—that is, board books—are not quick, easy reads. They are harbingers of bad parenting decisions to come.

One kind is the kind where you cut out a picture of your child's face and glue it to the book's pages so that she becomes the protagonist of her own story. You may be tempted to buy this kind of book.

And years later you may be tempted to place a bumper sticker on your minivan that announces to the world the strength of your daughter's academic prowess. Do neither of these things. It's not helping anybody.

What you should consider doing is purchasing *The Napping House*, *The Mitten* and *Goodnight Gorilla*. These are the good kind of board books. They are different from the kind that pretend to be books, but in reality turn out to be one big advertisement for a mass market breakfast cereal.

How these types of board books came to be is an utter mystery. Don't be part of the problem by buying them. Be part of the solution. Instead, try *The Carrot Seed*, *The Very Hungry Caterpillar* and *The Barnyard Dance*.

After all, there's nothing like a good book. Even a cardboard one with only one hundred words.

A Special Tribute to *Goodnight Moon*

As you've probably figured out by now, given those nine long months to think, plan, fret, rejoice and, of course, shop for your new bundle of joy, there are two kinds of "parental gear" in this world: that which is essential and that which is not.

You're likely already figuring out which is which. Extra binkies strategically placed throughout the home? Essential. Custom embroidered **BABY ON BOARD** sign for your vehicle? Not so much.

Most new parents are surprised to learn that a good portion of the junk designed to help with all the new burdens and responsibilities of being in charge of someone else's little life are, in fact, burdens in and of themselves. Yes, we're looking at you, electric bottle warmer—you are to new parents what the fondue set is to newly cohabitating couples. We think we'll need you, but in reality we don't. In both cases, that's what microwaves (and re-gifting) are for.

But for all the unessential parental gear cluttering the world that we find over time we don't really need, there are a few indispensable items that every new parent requires. It is our pleasure to introduce you to one of the most important. Moms and dads, let's all give a warm welcome and a big round of applause to . . . *Goodnight Moon.*

First published in 1947, Margaret Wise Brown's classic bedtime story is more than just "a book"—it's a nighttime mantra; a verbal security blanket for both you and your child. Allow us to explain:

In the great green room
There was a telephone
And a red balloon
And a picture of –
The cow jumping over the moon

So begins *Goodnight Moon,* one of the most famous bedtime stories of all time. As far as the plot goes, it's pretty straightforward. The author introduces a series of objects that can be found in "the great green room," and then one by one she—and by extension you and your child—wishes these various objects a very heartfelt goodnight.

The stuff of Shakespeare? Well, actually, yes. Like the Immortal Bard's "Sonnet number 20" (not to mention some of the best limericks ever constructed), *Goodnight Moon* is written in feminine rhyme (a prose scheme that matches two or more syllables at the end of respective lines.) Clocks and socks. Mittens and kittens. Bears and chairs. Your child will enjoy finding these objects as the ever-darkening illustrations and your own hushed tones will (hopefully) help soothe him or her into a peaceful slumber.

So there's that.

But that's not why we're giving this timeless classic its own special tribute. Let's talk frankly, parent to parent, shall we? This raising kids stuff is hard work. You already know that, of course, or at least have assumed it will be. We're just letting you know we're on the same page. And speaking of pages, at the end of a long day comprised of an endless procession of diapers and bottles and more diapers and naps taken and naps refused and unsolicited in-law advice and doctor visits, there's one thing left for you to do for your child before you can

steal a few precious moments for yourself (hooray!) and gear up for another long day ahead: you've got to read a bedtime story.

You're so close to some adult time you can practically taste it. All that's standing between you and that is the right book to help quickly and efficiently ease junior into the land of forty winks. And that's why *Goodnight Moon* is so essential. Not only does it lend itself to soothing your little one to sleep, it's only 130 words. That's it and that's all!

Before you know it, you'll have them all memorized. Soon, you won't even need the actual book. Instead, what you do is get your child all tucked in nice and cozy. Turn the lights down low. And then in a soft, still voice, begin ever so slowly and carefully using those 130 words to lull your child to sleep.

Thankfully, they're comforting words and quite often they do the trick the first time around. But there are those times when your child may require a little something extra to help him nod off. No problem. *Goodnight Moon* lends itself quite nicely to parental embellishment. Once the story is done, you can keep it going for as long as is needed by simply saying goodnight to whatever random crap you happen to see around you.

"Goodnight bottle warmer. Sorry I never took you out of the box." Or whatever. You get the point.

Goodnight, *Goodnight Moon*. Of all the essential parental gear, you are among the essentialest.

Where the Wild Things Are: So Good, It's Scary

Maurice Sendak's *Where the Wild Things Are* is the story of a mischievous boy and his vivid imagination. It's one of the most famous books in all of children's literature. For children, it can be a bit scary. For parents, it can be downright terrifying.

But despite, or maybe because, the book has a way of unsettling parents in a way that's hard to pin down, we keep reading because, well, we're supposed to, right? After all, it's award-winning. It's edgy. It's famous!

A snippet of conversation from *The Art of Maurice Sendak* between the author and a concerned parent illustrates the point:

Mother: Every time I read the book to my daughter, she screams.

Sendak: Then why did you continue reading it to her when she does not like it?

Mother: She ought to, it's a Caldecott book.

Caldecott, by the way, is the name of the literary award featured prominently on the book's cover. It's a literal seal of approval. But this little gold medal also represents an age-old parental conundrum: Should parents read this celebrated work of literature to their children in an effort to enrich their young lives? Or should they skip it altogether in an effort to, you know, keep their wee ones from getting the crap scared out of them?

The answer, we suggest, lies in how you "read" this read.

There are two very different ways to interpret the underlying message of *Where the Wild Things Are*. Just how scary the book is depends on which one you choose.

Boiled down to its essence,

Where the Wild Things Are is the story of a boy named Max being punished for causing "mischief of one kind and another." He is sent to bed without his supper and soon imagines a world filled with monstrous creatures. If one interprets the unseen mother's punishment as a "time out" rendered in the name of responsible parenting to teach the boy a lesson about self-control, then his subsequent adventures in trying to control the wild things—in other words, his attempt to wrestle with his own symbolic demons—becomes a metaphor for the benefits of strict parental guidance.

On the other hand, if you view the unseen mother as an absent parent whose aloof and destructive parenting actually causes the boy's negative behavior and symbolic demons, then the book becomes something else entirely.

And that's why *Where the Wild Things Are* is so great and so damn scary. The author simultaneously presents evidence for both sides. And while children might not understand what exactly it is about the book that frightens them, they know that somehow it does.

From the very first spread, the reader is presented with conflicting messages. Is Max a typical boy causing age-appropriate mischief, or is his behavior a form of a far greater dysfunction? That all depends on whether or not the Teddy Bear we see hanging from a rope is, like, "hanging" from a rope.

On the second spread, we see Max chasing a dog with a fork in his hand. Is he simply being a bit naughty and teasing his pet, or does he have something way more malicious in mind?

On the third spread, his mother calls him "WILD THING!" and sends him to bed without anything to eat. Is mom a responsible parent or is she, like, evil? It probably comes down to the tone of her voice when she uses those particular words. But since it's us, the reader, who supplies that tone, it's hard to know the author's intent.

And so it goes throughout the book. Even the wild things themselves are drawn as sort of a visual contradiction: they are oddly cuddly looking and frightening at the same time.

And that's why *Where the Wild Things Are* is scary as hell. Just how scary depends on how you read it.

A Special Dissing of
The Tale of Peter Rabbit

There are certain things in life that get better with the passing of time: wine, for example. Much tastier with a few years under the ol' cork. Capra movies. They just seem to improve with the turning of every calendar. Jeremy Piven's hairline. Seriously, it's never looked better.

Then there are those things that initially seem pretty great but lose some of their luster as they age. Such is the case with Beatrix Potter's *The Tale of Peter Rabbit*. When it was first published in 1902, it captured young readers' imaginations and sold millions of copies in the years that followed.

Rereading the story today, however, one can't help but feel . . . well, freakin' terrified! *The Tale of Peter Rabbit* is essentially a horror story.

Example: "'Now my dears,' said old Mrs. Rabbit one morning, 'you may go into the field or down the lane, but don't go into Mr. McGregor's garden: your Father had an accident there; he was put in a pie by Mrs. McGregor. Now run along, and don't get into mischief. I am going out.'"

That's right. You read that correctly.

Now imagine reading that sentence to your three-year-old at bedtime.

We tried it, once. It wasn't pretty.

By the way, in case you're wondering, Peter ignores this advice. He goes into Mr. McGregor's garden, and the rest of the story pretty much follows Mr. McGregor's failed attempts to murder the young cottontail.

Sleep tight, children everywhere!

Wait, You Didn't Say This Book Was Going to Be on the Test

Answer the following questions and you'll quickly know whether or not you are up to speed on contemporary kids' classics:

1. Complete the title:
a. *Chicka Chicka Boom* _____.
b. *Brown Bear, Brown Bear, What Do You* _____?
c. *The Saggy, Baggy* _____.
d. *Richard Scarry's Best* _____ *Ever*.
e. *Blueberries for* _____.

2. Which of the following is not used to describes Alex's day?
a. Horrible
b. Very Bad
c. Unbearable
d. No Good

3. When *Miss Nelson is Missing,* the substitute teacher is Miss Viola _____.

4. The chefs in Maurice Sendak's *In the Night Kitchen* resemble what classic movie comic:
a. Charlie Chaplin
b. Stan Laurel
c. Oliver Hardy
d. Lou Costello

5. Which Chris Van Allsburg book came first, *Zathura* or *Jumanji*?

6. Many highly respected literary figures have written children's

books. And many of these same people have written adult books that sound like they might be children's books. We'll name an author and two books. Your task: determine which is the children's book and which one is for adults:

Amy Tan
The Joy Luck Club
The Moon Lady

John Updike
Rabbit Run
A Child's Calendar

Joyce Carol Oates
Big Mouth & Ugly Girl
Where Are You Going, Where Have You Been?

Maya Angelou
My Painted House, My Friendly Chicken, and Me
Even the Stars Look Lonesome

7. In *A Year with Frog and Toad* and its sequels, which is taller, Frog or Toad?

8. According to the Laura Numeroff book, a long chain of events will result *If You Give a Mouse a* _____.

9. What is the given name of the Mike who operates a steam shovel?

10. What sort of animal is the passive Ferdinand?

11. What's odd about the title characters in *The Borrowers?*

12. Buckaroo is a horse. Rosetta is a rat. In the same book, what's *Corduroy?*

13. In the interactive classic *Pat the Bunny,* what is a child pretending to do when he or she sticks a finger through a hole in the book?

14. John Burningham's Mr Gumpy: Nice guy or mean guy?

The Worstiest Worst
of Dr. Seuss

We love Dr. Seuss. Really. He's written and illustrated some of the best children's books of all time. In fact, we pay tribute to him with his very own section later.

But something that we've rarely heard said is that the good doctor didn't always hit the ball out of the literary park. In fact, occasionally he was literally boring. And since his death, books have been put out under his name that we suspect the Doc would not have wanted his name on.

In light of his other achievements, though, we like to see the following duds not as anything that lessens his genius but just as indication that he was, in fact, human after all.

BARTHOLOMEW AND THE OOBLECK

This sequel to *The 500 Hats of Bartholomew Cubbins* has little of the forward motion of even Seuss's mid-level books. What it does have is thick prose, a been-there plot (smart kid tries to clean up after dumb king's wish is granted), and a dud of an ending.

THE SEVEN LADY GODIVAS

If it looks like a children's book and reads like a children's book, chances are that people are going to think it's a children's book, which this really isn't. The problem isn't the cartoon nudity that you'd expect from a title that references the famous story that redefined the word *bareback*. The problem is that it holds no interest for kids and just as little for adults. And the language isn't particularly playful or Seussian.

HOORAY FOR DIFFENDOOFER DAY

An alleged Dr. Seuss book based on some sketches and fragments of verses discovered by Geisel's secretary after his death. The literary equivalent of those Pink Panther movies that were made using discarded Peter Sellers footage. Okay, so it's not that bad. But it's really more of a lame *Stinky Cheese Man* book than a decent Seuss book.

DAISY-HEAD MAYZIE

The book cover announces "by Dr. Seuss," but anyone who's read any vintage Seuss will recognize the artwork as a fake. And the text, most of which was supposedly found in his drawer when he died, is subpar. It would be fine if this were, say, a lost James Joyce story published for the benefit of scholars. But this crappity-crap is given a spot in libraries and bookstores indistinguishable from the real thing.

ANY SEUSSISH BOOK BY BONNIE WORTH AND ARISTIDES RUIZ

They might be wonderful people, but these two have their names pinned to many books that cannibalize the Seuss legacy. With titles such as *Oh the Things You Can Do That Are Good For You!: All About Staying Healthy* umbrella'd under "Cat in the Hat's Learning Library," these knockoffs take the anarchic cat and turn him into a feeble educator.

The Grover Library

One of the inexplicable and unheralded realities of the Sesame Street world is that while some of its book spinoffs are educational, some are fun, and some are both, the only ones that are truly outstanding books that you'll want to read again and again are those featuring the furry blue monster, Grover.

We're not talking about the Healthy Happy Monster pabulum that has recently been put out in the great one's name. We're talking about the classics: *The Monster at the End of This Book, Another Monster at the End of This Book, Please Do Not Open This Book, Would You Like to Play Hide & Seek in This Book With Lovable, Furry Old Grover?* (all by Jon Stone and Michael Smollin), and the masterpiece *Grover and the Everything in the Whole Wide World Museum* (Norman Stiles, Daniel Wilcox, and Joe Mathieu).

In all, the barely-able-to-contain-himself charmer proves a master of getting kids—and parents—to ache to see what's on the next page. The authors and illustrators know just the right balance of text and illustration—and how to break with conventions and address the reader directly.

Now, we realize that Grover never quite got the attention that other core, original Sesame Street characters have garnered. Asked to recite the original Sesame Street Muppets and the average person is likely to fire off Ernie, Bert, Kermit, Cookie Monster, Big Bird (if you are including nonpuppet Muppets), and Oscar the Grouch first. Then there might be a pause. Then and only then might you hear Grover . . . and even then he might come after The Count.

Yet Grover's are the only *Sesame Street* books you really need in your library.

Books

25 Reasons Why Celebrities Should Not Write Children's Books

(and Why You Should Avoid Them)

25. Celebrities do things like go out in public without underpants and espouse their unsolicited political opinions and star in listless television sitcoms. Are these really the people you want writing books for your child?

24. You can write a book and call it *Sex* or you can write books for children but, sorry Madonna, you cannot do both.

23. Despite seemingly good intentions, their "messages" just confuse kids (and their parents) even more. Yes, we're looking at you Maria Shriver and your book's crazy animal heaven/people heaven theory. "There's a small white fence that separates them. During the day the people and the animals can play together if they want, but at night the animals have to stay in animal heaven and the

PART I: BOOKS ✳ **33**

people have to stay in people heaven." Oh, really? We must have skipped that part of the Bible.

22. They often dedicate the book to their own children then promptly name the characters after them. As such, it often feels like the story is written exclusively for their kids and not yours.

21. Even worse, they sometimes make *themselves* the lead characters. Let's see, kids, what book should we check out today? There's *Curious George* and here's *The Very Hungry Caterpillar.* Wait! Call in the dogs, the hunt it over: NFL superstars Tiki and Ronde Barber in . . . *Teammates.* Jackpot!

20. "Your mom is my daughter, and your dad is his mom's son. You lived within your mommy, but now the time has come. Get ready, sweet little one—your life will be just great. I'm going to be your grandpa, and . . . I can hardly wait." It's a sweet sentiment,

Billy Crystal, it really is. Now, how about turning this sentence over to a real writer for de-awkwardification.

19. Hey, John Travolta. We get that you're really, really, really into airplanes. You won't shut up about them. You named your kid Jett, for crying out loud. But if you think we're going to buy your book *Propeller One-Way Night Coach* so we can spend time showing our kids how much you really, really, really love airplanes, you're out of your freakin' mind.

18. *Jag's New Friend* by LeAnn Rimes.

17. "The tooth fairy envelope depicted in this book is a replica of the one my family uses. You may order them at toothfairyenvelopes.com." –Jason Alexander.

16. A recycled comedy routine (see especially Jerry Seinfeld's *Halloween* and Mel Brooks and

Carl Reiner's *The 2000 Year Old Man Goes to School*) is not an original children's book–it's, well, a recycled comedy routine.

15. "Maybe, if you are alone, in the privacy of your own home or bathroom, and not in a car, on a bus, in a plane, in school, on the roof, in the office, watching TV, in the movies, or on an elevator, it may be the only time . . . you can stick your finger up your nose. But don't let anyone see!" –Whoopi Goldberg, from *Whoopi's Big Book of Manners*. Somewhere, Dr. Seuss is sighing.

14. "Alan Arkin is an Oscar-winning and Tony-award winning actor, director and writer. Arkin has authored six books for children, including *The Lemming Condition*, which was chosen for inclusion in the White House Library." Where, hopefully, it will continue to stay, unavailable to the general public.

13. *New York State of Mind* by Billy Joel. The "story" is simply the lyrics to a song he wrote . . . thirty years ago.

12. *Flanimals* by Ricky Gervais. Ok, fine. *Even More Flanimals* by Ricky Gervais? Really, once was fine.

11. While Spike Lee and his wife Tonya (thankfully) tag-teamed the writing of their book, the world (and its children) saw no such generosity from Will Smith and Jada Pinkett Smith who decided that the world (and its children) needed books from them individually.

10. Because at last count Dr. Seuss's work is still in print.

9. Ditto Shel Silverstein.

8. And Eric Carle.

7. *Counting Blessings* by Debbie Boone.

6. "I Don't Want to Sleep Tonight *came into being as a poem I wrote for one of my sons*."–Deborah Norville "What I'd really like, Mom, is to borrow the car keys/See you later can I have them please?"

5. Almost all celebrities are not named Jamie Lee Curtis.

4. Or John Lithgow.

3. Or Dr. Cosby.

2. For every celebrity book that is published, a book by a professional children's author is not. At least, we think it works that way.

1. Kids only care about the quality of the story–not who wrote it.

A Few Celebrity-Authored Books That Are Actually Quite Good

As a rule, celebrity authors have no business writing children's books (see reasons why in the previous section). But every rule has its exceptions. Here are four (and no, we're not going to speculate on which had ghostwriters or heavy editors and which didn't).

THE SISSY DUCKLING BY HARVEY FIERSTEIN

Elmer is a little different than the rest of the boy ducks in the pond. While they play sports, he likes to bake. While they build forts, he puts on puppet shows. Because he's unlike the other ducks, they call Elmer a "sissy." His disapproving dad doesn't understand why Elmer can't just be like the other boys. Fortunately, his mom sees the bigger picture. She tells him: "You are special, Elmer, and being special sometimes scares those who are not."

Thus begins Harvey Fierstein's wonderful story about a little duck struggling to stay true to himself despite his community's preconceived notions of how they think he should be. Whereas many celebrity-authored books present their narratives in stilted rhymes, Fierstein presents his engaging "duck tale" through straightforward yet clever storytelling, accompanied by colorful illustrations from Henry Cole.

Given that the book is authored by the famously flamboyant Fierstein, it would be easy to assume its message is simply that "effeminate ducks" are every bit as special as "masculine ducks." But that would be a mistake. The book also examines father issues, bullies, and prescribed notions of gender identity—all of which add up to an examination of society's ingrained prejudices. Heady stuff for a children's book, to be sure. And in the hands of a lesser author, it might have come off too preachy or too dark to hold a child's interest. But Fierstein strikes just the right blend of whimsy, woe, and wonder, and the result is a book you'll want to read to your child again and again. In short, this book is simply ducky!

Tell your kid the author is the voice of Yao in *Mulan* and *Mulan II* and the Easter bunny in the Emmy Award–winning *Elmo Saves Christmas*.

THE REMARKABLE FARKLE MCBRIDE BY JOHN LITHGOW

Oh, pity the prodigy,
  Farkle McBride!
No matter what instrument poor
  Farkle tried,
Whether strumming,
Or blowing,
Or drumming,
Or bowing,
His musical passions were
  unsatisfied.

And so begins John Lithgow's tale of a young musical genius who just can't make up his mind as to which note-filled axe suits him best. Violin? Flute? Trombone? Drums? Farkle gives them all a try, and in the process young readers are taught that it's ok to experiment with different pursuits until you find the one that suits you best.

It's a nice message, but the real joy of this book (and for that matter all of Lithgow's books for children–see also *Marsupial Sue; I'm a Manatee;* and *Mahalia Mouse Goes to College*) is the author's love and use of language. Lithgow does more with a couple dozen words on a page than a couple dozen (wannabe) celebrity authors do with all their books combined. Throw in some fun illustrations by C. F. Payne and *Farkle* is indeed remarkable.

Tell your kid the author is the voice of Lord Farquaad in *Shrek* and the voice of Jean-Claude in *Rugrats in Paris.*

THE BEST WAY TO PLAY BY BILL COSBY

Little Bill and his friends want their parents to buy them a new video game based on their favorite TV show called *Space Explorers*. No luck on that, at least for Little Bill. So how are they supposed to have fun? By using their imaginations to create their own outdoor space adventures.

In this terrific book—part of a trilogy called "Little Bill Books For Beginning Readers"—Dr. Cosby teaches readers a valuable lesson about using media as a springboard for the imagination, not a substitute for it. The characters, like the story, are warm and accessible, and the book's message is clear but never comes across as an in-your-face sermon on the evils of modern media. We're not the only ones who admire this (and the other books in the series called *The Treasure Hunt* and *The Meanest Thing to Say*). To date these are the only children's books selected by Oprah's Book Club. With great illustrations from Varnette Hon Eywood, Little Bill is a big success.

When you're done reading, take in *Little Bill* the animated series on Noggin'. Oh, and when it's time to go all old-school, *Fat Albert and the Cosby Kids* and *The Electric Company* can be found on DVD featuring the talents of a younger Dr. Cos. But you probably already know all that.

Tell your kid the author is the dad on *The Cosby Show*. You do watch the reruns with your family, don't you?

TODAY I FEEL SILLY AND OTHER MOODS THAT MAKE MY DAY BY JAMIE LEE CURTIS

Today we feel jazzed. That's because we just reread Jamie Lee Curtis's bestselling examination of all the different moods that make up our kids' lives. From happy to sad and all emotional ports in between, the author brings wit and charm to her prose (even working diarrhea into the narrative without it seeming off-putting or weird). Plus, there's fun illustrations by Laura Cornell.

The plot finds a young female protagonist working her way through a variety of situations and reflecting on how these experiences make her feel. The message? "I'd rather feel silly, excited or glad, than cranky or grumpy, discouraged or sad. But moods are just something that happen each day. Whatever I'm feeling inside is ok!" Just as with her day job as a talented movie actress, Curtis's writing for children (see also *Where Do Balloons Go?* and *When I Was Little*) is both playful and real. In short, we predict the day you read this book to your child is a day (or a moment of it, anyway) you, too, will feel a bit jazzed.

Tell your kid the author is the voice of Queen Camillia in *Rudolph the Rednosed Reindeer and the Island of the Misfit Toys*. Actually, scratch that. Even your kid will recognize this DVD sucks. Instead, wait until Jr.'s fast asleep. Then rewatch the original *Halloween* (Curtis's first film role) and get the crap scared out of you all over again. C'mon, your whole day can't be filled with kids' stuff.

The Search is On: Hunting for Waldo et. al.

"It's time for bed. Go pick out a book," you say to your little one. And while you're planning on reading something relaxing, comforting, soothing . . . she returns with an oversized copy of *Where's Waldo?*, *I Spy*, or any of their copycat brethren.

This seems the appropriate time to state the obvious: some books just ain't meant for bedtime reading. Or for reading at all.

Some books are games. And while we applaud their ability to get kids to look between covers for enjoyment, we also must confess with the double-bind they tend to put us in. Specifically, our kids either a) become better than us at these, or b) get frustrated and cry, expecting us to be able to, in our parental wisdom, solve them on demand.

To that end, here are some strategies that may help you as you search for Waldo or whatever the book asks:

1. Despite the curves in the image, scan the pages from left to right.

2. Focus on color. Search for the red and white striped shirt and ignore everything else.

3. Decide first how you are . . . You know what? There really is only one strategy and that is this:

1 (revised). Take an hour *before* you give the kid the book and find the damn lost items in your own sweet time.

Noisy Books: "The Cow Says 'Moo.'" The Parent Says, "Throw This Damn Thing Against the Wall."

Some books have buttons.

When you read the text, you come to pictures that correspond to these buttons.

When you press these buttons, they make noise.

These books will drive you crazy.

These books have no artistic merit whatsoever.

We'd love to tell you to not buy them.

But we know such advice doesn't matter.

Noisy books have a way of finding their way into every room of your home.

How they got there is a mystery.

A present from "Nana and Pop-Pop?"

A birthday party parting gift you didn't notice?

They're, like, breeding?

Noisy books are the nosiest when you're not reading them.

Little hands have a way of pressing their buttons when you're making an important call.

Little hands have a way of pressing the same buttons over and over again.

Because you're on an important

call, there's nothing you can do about it.

"B is for ball."

"B is for ball."

"B is for ball."

"B is for ball."

You try to hide the noisy books from little hands.

You put them under your bed.

Just at that exact moment when the house is finally peaceful and you begin to nod off . . .

"B is for ball."

"B is for ball."

The noisy books are alive!

Or so it seems.

Noisy books have a way of "spontaneously talking."

It will scare the crap out of you.

You can't stop noisy books.

You can only hope to contain them.

Too Hip for the Pre-School: Post-Modern Kid Books

Ok, now who can tell us what the word *post-modernism* means? Anyone? Anyone at all?

No worries. You sing the alphabet song and "Itsy Bitsy Spider" enough times, you actually start to think like a toddler for a while. We've been there.

Anyway, loosely speaking, post-modernism is a term that is used to define forms that concentrate on surfaces rather than depths, challenge traditional values and aesthetics, and blur the distinctions between high and low cultures.

From philosophy to religion to technology, almost every discipline has a postmodern pioneer. Yes, even children's books have their "pomo" promoters.

One of the most recognizable authors of this brand of kid lit is Jon Scieszka. Some parents love his wink-wink reinterpretations of classic tales and his untraditional approach to entertaining and educating little ones. Other parents find his nonnarrative narratives confusing, smug, and, well, inappropriate for their precious bundles' wee little minds.

So who's right and who's wrong?

Well, from our point of view, it's . . . everybody. Herewith is a pros-and-cons rundown of three of Mr. Scieszka's most recognizable books:

THE TRUE STORY OF THE 3 LITTLE PIGS

About the book: Putting a modern-day spin on a classic tale about a troika of swine, their homes of varying practicalities, and a hungry wolf with a huge lung capacity, this version is told from the big bad one's point of view.

Pro: Teaches kids there are two sides to every story.

Con: Even though the first side is often the best.

Pro: Written by A. Wolf, which is kinda clever.

Con: Clever ain't exactly the highest priority on a four-year-old's storytelling agenda.

Pro: A reinterpretation of a classic tale often breathes new life into story time.

Con: Or, in this case, death: The wolf actually eats the first two little pigs.

Pro: Most parents, anyway, will find some measure of humor in seeing the wolf trying to defend himself against the "Big Bad Wolf" rap.

Con: Until, that is, he gets busted for attempting to break into the third pig's house and gets thrown in jail for attempted robbery. Maybe it's us, but what's particularly funny or instructive about that?

THE STINKY CHEESE MAN AND OTHER FAIRLY STUPID TALES

About the book: In this satirical update of several classic children's tales, including Little Red Riding Hood, Jack and the Beanstalk, and The Gingerbread Man, the author goes for laughs through self-reflexivity about the book's characters, structure, fonts, and other literary devices.

Pro: Great way to introduce your youngster to the poststructuralist concept of intertextuality and how it differs from straight-up parody.

Con: On second thought, that's what grad school is for . . . in twenty years. For now, it's fine to remain focused on the goal of teaching your child the importance of "making caca in the big-boy potty."

Pro: Quick, easy reads, won't easily lose a child's attention.

Con: These quick chapters won't necessarily capture a child's imagination, either. One of the running jokes is that some stories deliberately frustrate reader expectations by either abruptly ending the narrative or never really establishing a real plot to speak of. Groundbreaking idea for children's book? Check. Kind of interesting to parents the first read-through? Check. Confounding and sometimes maddening for kids? Double check.

Pro: Any way you slice it, saying the words "Little Red Riding Pants" never gets old.

Con: "Cinderumpelstiltskin." Not so much.

MATH CURSE

About the book: You can think of almost everything as a math problem. Pages of real and tongue-in-check examples ensue.

Pro: Aims to show that math can be cool.

Con: Fails.

Pro: Mitigates the thinkier parts with whimsical questions and problems like: "Why doesn't February have a w?" and "Estimate how many M&Ms you would eat if you had to measure the Mississippi River with M&Ms."

Con: Instead of a plot, there's, like, pages and pages of homework.

Enough Already: Disposable Kid Books

Visit just about any garage sale in any kid-populated area of America and you are likely to find not-quite-dog-eared copies from a book series about a dog with big ears. Specifically, a big red dog.

Underneath those "Clifford the Big Red Dog" books, you are likely to find other flimsy square paperbacks concerning the Berenstain Bears. And more about the moralistic adventures of a thing called Little Critter.

Why are these books so ubiquitous? And, more importantly, why are so many parents in a hurry to get rid of them? We've got some ideas.

First, these books were acquired cheaply—probably to shut up the cart-bound kid in the supermarket or while waiting for a prescription at the drug store. Their cheapness is a big part of the draw. If you are buying something simply to quiet down your kid, why not pick up the cheapest book on the rack? And a book is an easier purchase to rationalize than a Twix bar, easier to clean up after, and easier to ditch without buying if your kid loses interest before you reach the checkout counter.

Second reason these are easy to dispose of: they blur together. If you've got Little Critter's *Just Me and My Puppy, Just My Friend and Me* and *Just Shopping With Mom*, well, you're not going to see many tears if one ends up in the sale box on your lawn.

Third—with apologizes to Norman Bridwell, the author of the Clifford books—most of these just aren't very . . . good. The Berenstain Bears are particularly cloying. If you have an avid reading relationship with your kid, you'll soon want to move into something that hasn't been sequeled to death.

And you can get rid of the whole pile once your kid is savvy enough to ask "Hey, if their names are Papa Bear, Mama Bear, Brother Bear, and Sister Bear, what are the names of the bear family that lives down the block, huh? And what was Father Bear called before Mom popped the kids out?"

Books Based on Movie/TV Shows and Why to Avoid Them

Visit a bookstore or library and ask a kid to pick out a book, and he or she will almost invariably select something familiar. And familiar, for most kids, means something they've seen on TV or at the movies. That's human nature. We get that. It's why you don't find anthology shows like *Twilight Zone* on TV much anymore: Even as grown-ups, we are comforted by the things we already know.

As parents, though, we are in the unique position of having the power to steer our kids—for a few years, at least—away from the brand extensions and toward the good stuff. While they may reach for *Shrek the Third: The Junior Novel* or the *Bee Movie: The Honey Disaster,* we can declare a bedtime ban on such things and instead drive them toward *Goodnight Moon, Where the Wild Things Are, The Very Hungry Caterpillar* and other quality stuff. Trust us: if you've got other options around—and you hold a firm line—you won't get much resistance.

Is there anything inherently wrong with these books? Not really—except that there's nothing inherently *right* with them. Just try to read any of the Disney "Read-aloud Storybooks" three times without resisting skipping whole pages.

Ten Books to Know That We Couldn't Fit In Anywhere Else

1 *Blackberry Subway Jam.* Being a fan of Robert Munsch requires a fair amount of commitment. His books are written to be read with character and volume. Exaggerated faces are a must. So be forewarned. Truth is, we picked *Blackberry Subway Jam*–the story of a kid who finds out that there's a subway station in his closet–when we could have picked any of a dozen terrific Munsch-ers (*The Paper Bag Princess, Angela's Airplane, Pigs,* etc.). Just be careful about *I Love You Forever.* That breaking-the-Munsch-mold book isn't a silly lark but a tearjerker in the *Cats in the Cradle* vein.

2 *Daddy Makes the Best Spaghetti.* Anna Grossnickle Hines has a remarkable skill that we haven't seen in many other children's book authors–the ability to illustrate loving parents and grandparents who look as worn out as the loving parents and grandparents we know. Just look at the just-home-from-work mom in this sweet story–or the babysitting title character in Hines's *Grandma Gets Grumpy.*

3 *The Snowy Day.* Ezra Jack Keats's classic can be appreciated for its historical value. (It would be tough to find an earlier book, at least one nearly this popular, that features a young African-American boy as its central character.) But kids don't appreciate books for their historical value. And they shouldn't. For a young kid, *The Snowy Day* is a peaceful reinforcement of the magic of neighborhood.

4 *Clive Eats Alligators.* In this Allison Lester charmer, a category is introduced and we see the preference of each of seven friends. Actually, we first see six of them. Once your kid reads this and others in the series (*When Frank Was Four, Celeste Sails to Spain*) a dozen times or so, he or she will start guessing which one is missing. Thus, the book acts as a good read, a guessing game, and a subtle introduction to the idea that it's cool to have some different interests than your friends.

5 *Walter the Farting Dog.* The title says it all. Walter is a dog with a chronic issue. Life would be a gas if only he could stop his flatulence. He farts morning, noon, and night, and while the kids don't seem to mind, dad has had about enough. One more toot and Walter's getting the boot. Until, that is, some burglars show up and Walter's tummy troubles prove to be quite useful after all. Hidden in all of this is a nice, if irreverent, message about tolerance, understanding, and the power of a good air spray. It's also a good indication to new parents who haven't read a children's book since the Carter administration or earlier that, when it comes to children's book subject matter, the times they have definitely a'changed.

6 *Stellaluna.* When a baby fruit bat and her mother are attacked by an owl, young Stellaluna finds herself alone in a tree. Luckily, she befriends a mother bird and her three children. Soon, Stellaluna and the birds learn that, though they may come from different backgrounds, they have much they can learn from one another. With a gentle lesson about tolerance and lovely illustrations and text by Janell Cannon, *Stellaluna* shows us that friends can be found in the most unlikely places. And that bats aren't all bloodsuckers.

7 *Go, Dog, Go.* P.D. Eastman's ode to man's best friend is the whimsical story of a group of dogs engaging in a series of playful human activities (wearing hats, playing baseball, racing cars, etc.). Think of a literary version of "Dogs Playing Poker." Or Kerouac's *On the Road* with Labrador retrievers behind the wheel. The book's authorship is often misattributed to Dr. Seuss because Eastman (who was in fact a protégé of the good Doc) has a style that is very similar—but at his best is just as good as the master. If you ask us, there's just about nothing as enjoyable in all of children's literature as seeing the book's denouement—an elaborate dog party held on top of a tree.

8 *Flat Stanley.* When a bulletin board falls on him, Stanley Lambchop goes from a 3-D boy to a pancake-thin one. It's not all bad. Stanley serves as a kite for his younger brother, slides under closed doors, and even helps nab art thieves by hiding in a picture frame.

But as great as Jeff Brown's story is, perhaps its most notable literary legacy is that it inspired The Flat Stanley Project—an interactive literacy initiative where students from schools around the globe create their own Flat Stanleys and share their experiences with The Flat One in writing to each other.

9 *The Rainbow Fish.* Proud and vain, The Rainbow Fish thought he was better than all the other fish in the sea. And who could blame him? With his colorful shiny scales, he is indeed quite the looker. But when a little blue fish asks the Rainbow Fish for just one of his scales, the titular hero soon learns a valuable lesson about sharing and community involvement. That's the way we read it anyway. Some critics have suggested the book—written and drawn by Marcus Pfister—is a metaphor for socialism. Whatever. If you stare into the sea long enough you can find mermaids and giants monsters, too.

10 *A Day with Wilbur Robinson.* The Disney film *Meet the Robinsons* was okay, but it didn't quite capture the quirky charm of this William Joyce oddity about a lad's visit with his friend's unusual family. Think of it as *You Can't Take It With You* with singing frogs and sci-fi trappings. Joyce is one of those writers who knows how to put just enough words on the page. Joyce classics such as *George Shrinks, Dinosaur Bob and His Adventures with the Family Lazardo* and *The Leaf Men* are in the same vein—although he seems to have gotten sidetracked recently with the lesser *Rolie Polie Olie* stuff and movies such as *Robots*.

Intermezzo: The Wonderful Evolution of Oz

There are no figures in American literature more iconic than the characters created for the novel *The Wonderful Wizard of Oz*. But while the original books were the Harry Potters of their day—and while the stories' popularity spread across media—new parents are forgiven for not knowing much of the backstory.

Or for not knowing how many Oz stories there actually are.

Or for not knowing what the heck a Woggle-Bug is (more on that later).

But since this is the most iconic bit of kidlit of the last one hundred or so years, attention should be paid.

Here are just some of the high- and low-lights of the journey down the Yellow Brick Road:

1900: *The Wonderful Wizard of Oz* by L. Frank Baum and illustrated by the just-as-well-known-at-the-time W. W. Denslow is published (with the two splitting royalties). It proves to be the best-selling children's book of the year. And it still holds up in its original (beware of many abridged editions and rewrites out on the market). If you only know the MGM movie, you might be surprised at how much happens between the liquidating of the Wicked Witch of the West and the return to Kansas. And that the shoes are silver, not red. Oh, and by the way, it *wasn't* all a dream.

1902: The first theater production of *The Wizard of Oz* opens in Chicago. It's so successful that within a few weeks Fred Stone (the Scarecrow) and Dave Montgomery (the Tin Woodsman) are the best-known comedy team in the country.

1903: The stage version of *The Wizard of Oz* opens in New York City. Despite mixed reviews, it goes on to be the longest running show of the decade.

1904: The first Oz sequel, *The Marvelous Land of Oz,* is published. Dorothy is nowhere to be found in it. Neither is W. W. Denslow, who declared himself king of his own island in Bermuda (he made a few bucks from the first book and the stage production). The new illustrator is John R. Neill, who will continue as the illustrator of Oz for more than forty years. The biggest surprise in *Marvelous Land:* in a *Crying Game*–like twist, the young lead character, Tip, discovers in the end that he is actually a she. In fact, he's Princess Ozma of Oz.

That same year, Baum's "Queer Visitors from the Marvelous Land of Oz" newspaper strip begins. Its main character is The Woggle-Bug, a "highly magnified" creature from the second novel. Parker Brothers releases The Woggle-Bug Game of Conundrums. Baum's song "What Did the Wogglebug Say?" is published.

1905: The stage play *The Woggle-Bug* opens in Chicago to bad reviews.

1907: Apparently realizing that he should focus on the young girl of the first book rather than the strange insect of the second, Baum's second Oz sequel, *Ozma of Oz,* tells the story of Dorothy's return to Oz. Apparently, she has had a makeover. Unlike the cutesy tyke created by Denslow, Neill's Dorothy is more in the Gibson Girl style of the era and looks about ten years older. She's also now blonde.

1908: Dorothy comes back again in *Dorothy and the Wizard in Oz.*

1909: *The Road to Oz* is published. The coolest thing about this book is that different colored pages are used to represent each land Dorothy visits. Some reprints keep to that style. Most don't.

1910: The first film version of *The Wonderful Wizard of Oz* is released. Meanwhile, Baum and Neill's *The Emerald City of Oz* is published. This time, Aunt Em and Uncle Henry join Dorothy in Oz, and Baum says it's his last Oz book.

1911: Baum's new children's fantasy, *The Sea Fairies,* is published. With this title, Baum attempts to launch a new fantasy series that he hopes will replace Oz. It does fine, but demand for Oz books is greater.

1913: It doesn't take Baum long to change his mind. *The*

Patchwork Girl of Oz is released. To this day, it's a favorite with Oz fans. The first edition of *The Little Wizard Stories* is also published. These are six short stories featuring the Oz characters, and even though some of the characters may be unfamiliar, it's a good book to introduce young readers to the stories.

1914: *The Patchwork Girl of Oz* is released as a film. So is *His Majesty, The Scarecrow of Oz.* It goes on like this for the next few years. More Oz books. More theater productions.

1919: L. Frank Baum dies. His book *The Magic of Oz* is released posthumously.

1920: Another Baum manuscript, *Glinda of Oz,* is released. Not wanting to end the series, Baum's publishers invite Ruth Plumly Thompson, best known for her book *The Perhappsy Chaps,* to take over as Royal Historian of Oz.

1921: Thompson's first Oz book, *The Royal Book of Oz,* is released with Baum's name on it. She continues with just about a book a year until . . .

1940: . . . she dies and illustrator John R. Neill takes a shot at both writing and illustrating Oz books. His first is *The Wonder City of Oz.* But, we're getting ahead of ourselves a bit. Back up to:

1925: Another film version of *The Wizard of Oz* is released. This one, written by Frank Baum Jr., features as the Tin Woodsman (a pre-Laurel-and-) Oliver Hardy. But the one you are waiting for is . . .

1939: MGM's *The Wizard of Oz* is released. "Over the Rainbow"– which was almost cut from the film–becomes a national hit and wins an Oscar for Best Song.

1946–1954: Jack Snow and, later, Rachel Cosgrove take over writing the Oz books. Snow's

1954 volume *Who's Who in Oz* doesn't tell a story but, rather, offers a dictionary of the Oz characters thus far.

1956: Something of a national holiday is launched when the 1939 film of *The Wizard of Oz* is broadcast on television for the first time. Around the same time, the original novel enters the public domain, which explains why so many versions of the book you see out there these days are absolute crap.

By this time, Disney has bought rights to the Baum Oz books. Some believe this is purely a defensive move. Three years later, Disney's plans to feature a Land of Oz area at Disneyland are scrapped.

1974: Liza Minnelli, daughter of Judy Garland, is the voice of Dorothy in the animated feature *Journey Back to Oz*. Ethel Merman, Milton Berle, and Mickey Rooney are also heard. Why does the talent all seem, well, of another generation?

Because the voice tracks were recorded in 1963–64, before financing for the film collapsed. A decade later, it hit theaters and then was shown on television. Jack Pumpkinhead and the wicked witch Mombi, both from Baum's *The Marvelous Land of Oz*, are featured, but little of the spirit of the books or the classic film (of which it was touted as a direct sequel to) are present. It's available on DVD. Don't bother.

1975: *The Wiz*, an African-American musical version of *The Wizard of Oz*, opens on Broadway. It's a hit. And it's got some terrific songs, including "Ease on Down the Road" and "Be a Lion." If your local high school is putting it on, check it out.

1978: A feature film version of *The Wiz* opens starring Michael Jackson as the Scarecrow and a long-in-the-tooth, thirty-four-year-old Diana Ross as Dorothy. While Richard Pryor doesn't make for a

very interesting wizard, Jacko's actually pretty good in it, but given subsequent events, it's difficult to stomach his starring in a kid's film.

1982: Science-fiction writer Philip Jose Farmer's *A Barnstormer in Oz* is published. It ain't for kids.

1985: Disney's live-action feature film *Return to Oz* opens. It's a colossal failure.

1991: *The Oz Squad* comics launch. One collector calls them "the most repellent published work with the name Oz in the title I have ever seen." It ain't for kids.

1992: *Was* by novelist Geoff Ryman is published. It focuses on the story of both Judy Garland and the "real" Dorothy. It ain't for kids either (there's a pattern forming here).

1993: The MGM Grand Hotel features a section built around an Oz theme. No matter what PR people at the time may have tried to sell you, Las Vegas isn't and never was for kids.

1995: *Wicked: The Life and Times of the Wicked Witch of the West,* by Gregory Maguire, is published. Boy, is this one not for kids. In one of the odder Oz moments of the century, Roger Daltry—of The Who fame—is the Tin Woodsman, and Jackson Browne is the Scarecrow in a concert version of the MGM movie. It's broadcast on TNT.

2003: *Wicked,* a musical version of Gregory Maguire's novel, is a huge hit on Broadway. The edge of the book is softened, making this particularly popular with teen and pre-teen girls. Don't take your kid to it yet.

2007: The Sci-Fi Channel premiers a science fiction series called *Tin Man*. This one isn't for your kids, either.

Part II

TV AND

VIDEO

And now we turn to television, which, if you believe what you read elsewhere, is like Satan babysitting your children. On the other hand, if you've had a kid for long enough, you know that sometimes you'll take just about any babysitter you can get.

It used to be that the problem was "kids watching all that junk." Now there's plenty of good stuff out there, so the question is more of quantity than of quality. It's very easy to find pretty good kids programming on TV just about any time of day. And you'll quickly acquire a library of DVDs of available-when-you-want-them choices to supplement your runs to the video stores, orders from Netflix, and trips to the library (where picking up a DVD has become as common as checking out a book).

That's a different world than weekday and Saturday mornings, which used to be the only times to find the good kid stuff.

Of course, that great kid programming can be two clicks away from an episode of The Sopranos or an afternoon airing of The Exorcist, so you still have to be careful.

We've combed through kid TV old and new to create the section that follows. In doing so, we've found a lot to celebrate and guide you toward—and some major obstacles to avoid.

12 Moments Where the Muppets Are as Great as Anything Ever Created by Mankind

You love them on *Sesame Street*. You dug their movies. (Well, at least a few of them. We weren't big on *The Dark Crystal* either.) And perhaps you were of age when *The Muppet Show* aired (it's available on DVD, perfect for the next home-with-the-sick-kid day).

No matter when or where you were exposed to this menagerie that sprang from the mind of Jim Henson and his cohorts, you are no doubt aware of their brilliance.

Here, then, is our selection of the Muppets' greatest hits:

1. Kermit the Frog singing "It's Not Easy Being Green." *(Sesame Street)*

2. Ernie singing "Dancing Myself to Sleep" and driving his roommate Bert crazy in the process. *(Sesame Street)*

3. Johnny Cash singing "Dirty Ol' Egg Suckin' Dog" with an offended Rowlf the Dog on piano. *(The Muppet Show)*

4. Kermit on the bicycle *(The Muppet Movie*–Yes, we're putting some films in the TV section. So sue us).

5. Ernie and Shawn Colvin singing "I Don't Want to Live on the Moon." *(Elmopalooza)*

6. Bert presiding over the meeting of the National Association of "W" Lovers. *(Sesame Street)*

7. The "Don't Forget to Watch the Movie" pre-movie short. (Lowe's Theaters)

8. The alien creatures doing the nonsensical "manamana song." *(The Muppet Show)*

9. Beaker singing "Feelings"– although the laugh track is annoying. *(The Muppet Show)*

10. Every page of *Grover and the Everything in the Whole Wide World Museum.* (see the Books section)

11. Ernie jamming to "Put Down the Duckie." *(Sesame Street)*

12. The moment when Statler and Waldorf join in with John Denver and the Muppets on "Home on the Range." *(The Muppet Show)*

The ABCs of Kiddie TV: An Abridged Encyclopedia

The alphabet book is a staple in kid libraries. Here, we use that format to introduce you to an A-to-Z of contemporary kids TV shows and characters that you've probably never heard of.

A IS FOR *ARTHUR*

Based on Mark Brown's *Arthur* book series, this PBS Kids show chronicles the life and times of an anthropomorphic aardvark named Arthur Read. As Arthur's last name suggests, the show has a strong emphasis on books and literacy. It also often deals with health and social issues (although not as radically as its spinoff series *Postcards From Buster*, which caused some controversy in a 2005 episode by showing Buster meeting several children of lesbian parents). One aspect of Arthur that makes the show appealing to parents is its frequent yet subtle pop culture references. *The Sopranos, Citizen Kane*, Oprah Winfrey, James Bond, and many other film and TV series and stars have been referenced in some way. Plus, the show's theme song, performed by Ziggy Marley, is one snappy little ditty.

B IS FOR *BOB THE BUILDER*

While Bob the Builder is a construction contractor overseeing a variety of renovations and repairs, he's really an expert in conflict resolution, helping his colleagues (and your little one) to understand the value of patience and cooperation when working through a problem. His signature catchphrase is "Can we fix it?" to which others around him respond "Yes we can!" Think of him as Bob Villa for preschoolers.

C IS FOR *CAILLOU*

Caillou is a wide-eyed (and bald) four-year-old with a curiosity about the world around him, turning his day-to-day activities into vivid adventures. This PBS Kids show, based on the books by author Christine L'Heureux and illustrator Helene Desputeaux, finds Caillou and his friends getting into and out of trouble with help from Caillou's wise mother Doris, bumbling father Boris, mischievous sister Rosie, and his kind grandparents. If nothing else, your kid learns that *L*s can be silent.

D IS FOR *DORA THE EXPLORER*

On *Dora the Explorer*, there's always a task at hand, a sense of optimism about taking it on and, well, some cool Spanish vocabulary words to be learned. In this Nickelodeon staple (also airing on Noggin'), Dora goes on a three-part quest with assists from pals Boots, Backpack, Map, and others. The biggest obstacle in their way: Swiper the Fox.

Little girls especially identify with Dora's go-getting attitude. But alas, every great lesson has its price. Dora merchandise is a billion-dollar-a-year industry. But, hey, buying your kid a stuffed Boots doll is a small price to pay for getting her interested in Spanish at an early age, right? Or, if she already speaks the language, for empowering her.

E IS FOR
EINSTEINS, LITTLE

Little Einsteins follows the adventures of four preschool smarty-pants who have preternatural skills in music and a love of art. Culturally significant works of art and music are integrated into the plots and soundtrack to help teach the toddler-plus about the finer things in life.

F IS FOR *FRANKLIN*

The titular turtle shows his audience how to solve problems on their own while at the same time showing that it's also ok to ask for help from mom and dad if needed. The show demonstrates the importance of participating in activities, games, and exercise. Franklin and his large circle of pals are frequently seen playing baseball, hockey, soccer, hide-and-seek, tag, and even chess—kind of what your kid *isn't* doing when he's watching the show.

G IS FOR
GO, DIEGO, GO

Diego Marquez is a brave, bilingual adventurer who spends his days saving animals in the rain forest. He's also the cousin of Dora the Explorer (sweet!) who sometimes makes cameos on his Nick Jr. series. If you hear your kid utter the words "Freeze, Bobos!" it's because he heard Diego catching the Bobo Brothers—a pair of spider monkeys—in a larcenous act.

H IS FOR
HIGGLYTOWN HEROES

A true hero, this Playhouse Disney series shows us, is often someone who lives right next door, whether it's firefighters, librarians, or dentists. Now here's the weird part—the show's main characters, Eubie, Wayne, Twinkle, Kip, and their pal Fran, a red squirrel, are modeled after Russian nesting dolls. Moving, in other words, is a bit awkward. Some parental pluses: good celeb guest voices, including Cindy Lauper, Sharon Stone, Ed McMahan, and Tim Curry. Plus a catchy theme song performed by They Might Be Giants.

I IS FOR *IT'S A BIG, BIG WORLD*

On Playhouse Disney's *It's a Big, Big World,* young, young viewers are introduced to a variety of different rain forest species that live in or around the World Tree. The main character is Snook, a sloth who's always up for a little scientific investigation (when he's not napping, that is). Each episode features two unrelated segments broken up by a song. At the end of each show, Snook provides some fun factoids on the species that live in the World Tree. No matter what *your* political persuasion, don't be surprised if your kid turns into a tree hugger.

J IS FOR *JOHNNY AND THE SPRITES*

"You never know what you can do, until you try something new" is the overriding principle behind Playhouse Disney's *Johnny and the Sprites.* And that motto could have applied to Johnny T (the show's creator and producer John Tartaglia), who went from starring in the raunchy-puppets-on-Broadway hit *Avenue Q* to this song-and-dance show. Even if your kids become big fans of Johnny, you might not want to let junior sing along to *Avenue Q's* "It Sucks to Be Me."

K IS FOR *KENNY THE SHARK*

Tired of ocean life, Kenny—a tiger shark—decides to make a life for himself on land. His best pal is a young girl named Kat, who is the only human who can speak Kenny's language. This Discovery

Kids series is more focused on delivering comedic entertainment than it is on delivering big moral messages. Then again, there wasn't much morality in *Jaws* either.

L IS FOR *LAZYTOWN*

"Get up, get out of the house, and play" is the message of *LazyTown*. The star of this Nick Jr. show is an active and pink-clad eight-year-old girl named Stephanie, who just so happens to be the niece of LazyTown's mayor. Armed with the catchphrase "there's always a way," Stephanie wants to make her town's citizens more active and healthy. Her helper is a "slightly-above-average-hero" Sportacus. The villain is the junk food-loving and stasis-advocating Robbie Rotten. And, yes, we appreciate the irony of parking your kid in front of a television to watch a show that promotes exercise.

M IS FOR *MAX AND RUBY*

Based on Rosemary Wells's children's books, *Max and Ruby* centers on the problem-solving techniques of a rambunctious four-year-old bunny and his responsible older sister. Curiously, Max and Ruby's parents are never seen, but it's implied they are around, just not during the show's running time. Don't be upset if your pride and joy occasionally has those feelings about you.

N IS FOR NOGGIN'

Like its sister channel Nickelodeon, Noggin' is a cable television network with programming targeting the toddler to preschool set. It features classic Nick episodes from series like *Blues Clues* and *Dora the Explorer* as well as original programming like *Oobi and Jack's Big Music Show*. While programming runs commercial-free from 6 am to 6 pm, age-appropriate music videos and ads for fake products (Mud 'N Bugs Cereal) are shown between shows. We're not sure if fake ads are any better for kids than real ones.

O IS FOR
OOH & AAH

The official hosts of Playhouse Disney, Ooh and Aah are blue and red monkeys, respectively. These puppet pals appear during various segments after commercial breaks as well as in the short series *Ooh, Aah and You*. We're still waiting around for Urgh, Yuck and Yikes.

P IS FOR
PINKY DINKY DOO

Pinky is an imaginative seven-year-old city girl who uses her noggin to solve problems (literally—her head swells up when she comes up with a creative solution). Other main characters on this Noggin' series are Pinky's little brother Tyler and their pet, Mr. Guinea Pig. Each episode ends with an interactive segment where children watching at home are encouraged to make up their own stories. We think that's great, but we're still freaked about the head thing and would love to see an episode of *ER* dealing with a similar affliction.

Q IS FOR
QUALITY TIME WITH YOUR CHILD WITHOUT THE TV ON

Just a reminder.

R IS FOR
READING RAINBOW

This long-running PBS series focuses, not surprisingly, on the virtues of literacy and encourages reading. Moreover, book recommendations are provided, and each episode focuses on a particular book's theme. It's hosted by actor LeVar Burton who, depending on your generation, you will remember as either the star of *Roots* or the guy with the hair band over his eyes on *Star Trek: The Next Generation*.

S IS FOR *SAGWA*

Sagwa is not your typical children's show protagonist. For one, she is the creation of acclaimed novelist Amy Tan *(The Joy Luck Club),* who is best known for her books for adults. For another, Sagwa is part of a royal family of cats who lives in a palace in China. Because the show is set in the early 1900s and in an exotic locale, it teaches children about the importance of history while promoting awareness of other ethnicities. And admit it, your knowledge of Chinese history is limited to what you learned on soup-stained paper placemats.

T IS FOR *TELETUBBIES*

Tinky Winky. Dipsy. Laa-Laa. Po. Say hello to the *Teletubbies*. These four toddlerlike creatures live in the idyllic Teletubbyland, where the sky is almost always blue and the sun is almost always shining. Each Teletubby has a video screen on his or her belly that helps segue into short film clips. The *Teletubbies* speak in a garbled baby language and their day-to-day activities are presented at a slow pace. Unlike most children's shows, the *Teletubbies* don't really have a lesson they want to teach or difficult problem they need to solve. Rather, they simply want to celebrate the wonder and joy that comes with being little.

That said, being a Teletubby isn't always easy. In 1999 evangelical pastor Jerry Falwall stirred up some controversy when he accused Tinky-Winky of being a homosexual symbol.

Oh, and don't think you've lost your mind: each video sequence is repeated twice in each episode.

U IS FOR *UPSIDE DOWN SHOW, THE*

Starring physical comedians The Umbilical Brothers (Shane Dundas and David Collins), Nick Jr.'s *The Upside Down Show* is one of the more parent-friendly children's programs on TV. Each episode finds our hosts in search of a new room in their apartment with the aid of children at home using imaginary remote controls to help guide Shane and David by pressing buttons (to great comic effect). Their journey takes them through several wrong turns, and the kids at home learn the importance of persistence and curiosity.

V IS FOR VARIOUS SHOWS WE HAVEN'T MENTIONED YET

Here are a few: *Between the Lions, Boohbah, Dragon Tales, Handy Many, My Friends Tigger & Pooh* and *Mickey Mouse Clubhouse.*

W IS FOR *WONDER PETS*

Teamwork is the focus of this Nick Jr series, but what really separates it from other shows is that a good portion of the dialogue is sung: a live orchestra scores each episode and the animation style is called "photo-puppetry." And it's lasted longer than *Cop Rock* and *Viva Laughlin* combined.

X IS A KIND OF SHOW OR DVD FOR MOM AND DAD

After your precious lil' angel has been tucked in, of course.

Y IS FOR *YO GABBA GABBA*

With its manic look and characters and absurd style of family-friendly humor, this Nick Jr series is designed to appeal as much to adults as it is to children. Not unlike *Peewee's Playhouse* before it, *Yo Gabba Gabba* features a variety of wild characters, including five toy monsters named Brobee, Foofa, Muno, Plex, and Toodee.

Z IS FOR *ZOBOOMAFOO*

Learning about both common and exotic animals is at the heart of this PBS Kids series. Children are encouraged to learn about a variety of furry and feathered friends by observing them in their habitats as they pass through Animal Junction, home to Zoboo, a wide-eyed lemur, and his human pals the Kratt brothers.

While the show teaches kids the importance of exploration, it also encourages them to be considerate, caring, and helpful to people and animals. We're too distracted trying to figure out the exact moments when puppet Zoboo turns into real-life Zoboo.

Sesame Test: This Quiz Has Been Brought to You by the Letter *Q*

1. What year did *Sesame Street* debut?

a) 1968   c) 1970

b) 1969   d) 1971

2. Contrary to popular belief, Big Bird is not a canary. He is, in fact, a

a) Golden condor

b) Yellow robin

c) Finch

d) Eagle

3. Which *Sesame Street* song peaked at #16 on the Billboard Hot 100 chart?

a.) "I Love Trash"

b.) "Doin' the Pigeon"

c.) "Mahna Mahna"

d.) "Rubber Ducky"

4. Match the character to its favorite thing:

Trash	Zoe
Triangles	Cookie Monster
Baths	Bert
Cookies	Telly Monster
Pigeons	Oscar
Pet Rock	Ernie

5. True or False: Snuffleupagus's first name is Aloysius.

6. Who is not an original cast member?

a) Bob

b) Gina

c) Gordon

d) Luis

7. *Sesame Street*'s resident magician is The Amazing Mumford. His trademark magic words are: _____.

8. Tickle Me Elmo was the hottest toy of this year:
a) 1994
b) 1995
c) 1996
d) 1997

9. Match the live character with his or her occupation:

Veterinarian	Bob
Music teacher	Gina
Science teacher	Luis
Nurse	Gordon
Proprietor of The Mail-It Shop	Susan

10. How tall is Big Bird?
a) 6'11"
b) 7'5"
c) 8'2"
d) 9'0"

11. This Muppet monster's alter ego is "smarter than a speeding bullet."
a) The Incredible Cookie Monster
b) Super Grover
c) Elmo the Fantastic
d) The Amazing Oscar

12. True or False: The little guys that live in Ernie's flowerbed are called Twiddlebugs.

13. Who had a baby on Sesame Street?
a) Maria
b) Gina
c) Susan
d) The Count

14. The names Ernie and Bert were inspired by characters from this movie classic:
a) *Casablanca*
b) *Citizen Kane*
c) *It's a Wonderful Life*
d) *Gone With the Wind*

15. How old is Elmo?
a) 3
b) 3 ½

c) 4

d) 4 ½

16.Who is the host of "Monsterpiece Theater"?

A) Telly Monster

B) Herry Monster

C) Prairie Dawn

D) Cookie Monster

17. Add the missing lyrics to the _Sesame Street_ theme song. "Sunny day/Sweepin' the clouds away/on my way to _____.

18. True or false: Oscar's fur has always been green.

19.Which of the following is _not_ among Bert's interests?

a) Pigeons

b) Bottle caps

c) Paper clips

d) Rubber bands

20. Jim Henson created the original Kermit the Frog out of his mother's

a) Drapes

b) Purse

c) Coat

d) Bedspread

21. Guy Smiley is America's favorite

a) Game show host

b) Weather man

c) Math teacher

d) Super genius

22. True or False: A pig, worm, elephant, and dog are all pets of Oscar.

23. This character was deliberately created to complement Elmo:

a)Benny Rabbit

b)Curly Bear

c) Baby Bear

d) Zoe

24. This _Sesame Street_ guest star performed the song "Rebel L"

_____.

25. True or False: Elmo was among the original cast of muppets.

Barney and Friends vs. *Bear in the Big Blue House*

(With an Assist from The Teletubbies*)*

Several years ago, conservative pundit cum culture critic Reverend Jerry Falwell grabbed a few headlines and caused a bit of a stir when he suggested that when it comes to children's television, there are deeper meanings and messages than initially meet the eye.

Specifically, he accused one of the *Teletubbies*—a PBS show aimed at the youngest of viewers—of being "homosexual." The character Tinky-Winky, after all, was armed with a handbag and was noted for his triangular antennae (triangles apparently being the "gayest" of all shapes).

Some parents got mad, taking refuge in the "it's just a children's program" defense. Other parents agreed with the Rev.

As it turns out, both sides were probably right. On the one hand, c'mon, there are bigger problems in the world that need solving. On the other hand, we have watched *Teletubbies* dozens of times and we still have no idea what the hell is going on in Teletubby Land save this: Tinky-Winky is so flaming it's a wonder he hasn't spontaneously burst into a fireball.

Yep, he's gay. And good for him.

But there's a bigger point to be made here. There are two messages that a good deal of children's television presents: The one on the surface meant for the target audience. And the sneakier one that lurks just behind it.

Let us consider two popular children's shows of a few years back—*Barney and Friends* and *Bear in the Big Blue House.*

At first blush, these shows seem somewhat similar in their ostensible agendas. But a careful analysis reveals that their deeper messages could not be more different.

Ever since The Big Purple One first began popping up on millions of small screens across the country in the early 1990s, Barney-bashing has become a kind of parental rite of passage right up there with learning to earnestly utter the words "poopy diaper" sans irony. The very qualities that make Barney such an appealing icon to youngsters are also the qualities that cause many adults to loathe him with white-hot intensity. What sends them over the top? Take your pick: his makes-you-want-to-incite-a-riot giggle; his "Super-de-duper"; or the maddening way he utters the most mundane

sentences with the aw-shucks glee of a former blind man seeing the world for the first time (e.g. "It's yum, yum, pumpernickel bread!")

But if you watch enough *Barney* episodes—and since you've brought a child into this world and most likely own a television, chances are you will—you'll see that beneath all the prancing and sing-song and baked goods hyperbole, Barney is all about extolling the virtues of conformity.

Parents hate conformity. Young kids crave it. They play follow-the-leader for a reason.

Which brings us to Bear, *of Bear in the Big Blue House* fame.

Bear is not just one of the best children's programs out there—it's also one of the most parent-friendly. Why? Well, Bear is actually kinda, sorta . . . cool. That is to say, of all the small-screen kiddie heroes around, Bear is one of a very small minority we'd like to go grab a beer with after work. Because Bear is to making the rules what Barney is to following them.

TV and Video

Like Kierkegaard, and Nietzsche before him, Bear is an existentialist nonpareil. You may recall from that college philosophy class that an existentialist is one who concerns himself with making his own choices and living with the consequences. Such concerns are what a good chunk of parenthood and, indeed, childhood is about.

Unlike Barney, however, Bear does not necessarily suggest there is a right and wrong way to tackle life's challenges. For in the Big Blue House, as in life, there often is no right and wrong–there just is.

To be specific: Whereas Barney presents the act of brushing teeth as having a specific set of rules and an order of operations ("Oh, I'm brushing my teeth on top/I'm having so much fun I can't stop/But while I'm brushing my teeth and having so much fun/I never let the water run, no/I never let the water run."), for Bear oral hygiene is an experience notable for its spontaneity and lack of structure. In the song/set piece "Brush Brush Bree," Bear and his friends individually tell the viewer that "My favorite thing about brushin' my teeth is 'Zhucka-Zhuka-Zhuka-Zhucka-Zhucka-Zhuka-Zhuka-Zhucka.'" Put another way, for the inhabitants of the Big Blue House, dental care is enjoyable for the very sounds of the experience, the very smells of the experience ("Mmm! Do you always smell this good when you Brush Brush Bree, Brush Brush Broo."), the spontaneity of the experience ("Look, Pop, I just found a clam").

Brushing one's teeth is an experience, not a right-or-wrong chore.

Take another example. In "Potty Time with Bear," Bear says, when asked what he's been up to that day, "For some reason we're discussing using the potty." "For some reason"–as if the issue just came up and was not part of a larger predetermined agenda. In other words, in the Big Blue House as in life, literally and figuratively . . . shit happens. Unlike Barney, when Bear is sorting through an issue, he doesn't offer many steadfast rules—he simply tries to help his young friends make sense of life's challenges.

So there you have it. Two similar shows. Two very different agendas. One celebrates conformity. The other celebrates existentialism.

Having deconstructed these messages, it's now up to you to decide which show is right for your child.

Now, let's take a look at the word *codependence* and examine its relationship to *Sesame Street*'s Ernie and Bert . . . actually, scratch that. Enough of this heady stuff.

Let's call Bear and see if he's available for cocktails.

Superhero Substitutions

Some run faster than speeding bullets. Others fight evil galactic empires. More than a few are mutants. And at least one is a vigilante billionaire with deep psychological issues (and nifty gadgets!)

Their images are in fast food kid meals. Their toys are in stores. So it stands to reason that your kid will want to see them on the big screen. Or at least on your more modest screen.

But many superhero movies are rated PG-13 – as in "age 13 and up is probably the audience these movies are best suited for."

On the one hand, you've already implicitly validated your child's interest in this stuff by allowing him to play with superhero toys and buying him the Halloween costume of his favorite hero.

On the other hand, Batman is called "The Dark Knight" for a reason. He's a brooding badass who packs a serious punch. And that evil Lord of the Sith Darth Vader isn't likely to be making a cameo appearance on *Sesame Street* anytime soon.

What to do?

Fear not. We've scoured Gotham, Metropolis, Tatooine and beyond for age-appropriate home viewing alternatives to the PG-13 options you don't yet feel comfortable introducing to your 3–6 year old.

BATMAN

Since his first appearance in *Detective Comics* #27 (May 1939) the Bat-Man (as he was first known) has become increasingly more complicated. In more recent years, thanks to Frank Miller's graphic novel *The Dark Knight Returns* and the Christopher Nolan–directed movie *Batman Begins,* The Dark Knight just seems to keep getting darker.

While these takes on Bruce Wayne and his nighttime alter ego are captivating for adults, they are probably not ideal for the 3-to-6 set, so . . .

Instead Try: *Batman: The Animated series.* This Emmy Award–winner is regarded by many Dark Knight enthusiasts as the best of all the attempts to capture the true essence of the Caped Crusader on the small screen. While the series, now available on DVD, is partially inspired by Tim Burton's big screen take on Batman and contains a bit more violence than traditionally found in animation aimed at children, such action (punching, kicking, and the occasional discharged firearm) is not as graphic or disturbing as that which can be found on its big screen counterparts. If this doesn't work for you, let him watch the tongue-in-cheek Adam West/Burt Ward series—or the movie that was spun off from it.

STAR WARS

A long time ago, in a galaxy far, far away (northern California to be exact), George Lucas conceived one of the most original and enduring film franchises in the history of the medium; a little something called *Star Wars.*

While the series began as more or less a family-friendly enterprise, oddly enough, as the franchise aged, it seemed to increasingly skew to younger audiences. Until, that is, the final installment of the series—*Revenge of the Sith*—was released, bringing some very adult closure to the Skywalker family's dysfunctional space saga.

Sith, with its beheading of the evil Count Dooku, graphic disfiguring of the even eviler Emperor Palpatine, and the even-uncomfortable-for-adults near-death-for-Darth lava pit

sequence, is the last of the *Star Wars* films and the only one to garner a PG-13 rating. So . . .

Instead Try: *Star Wars: Clone Wars.* This Emmy Award–winning animated series, which first appeared as a recurring series of shorts on Cartoon Network and is now available on DVD, features many of the characters and themes found in *Revenge of the Sith.* Set in the three-year period between the last two *Star Wars* films, *Clone Wars* is heavy on action but goes much lighter on *Sith*'s darker themes.

SUPERMAN

O f all the heroes in the comic universe who have found their way onto the silver screen, the movies starring The Man of Steel are arguably the safest bets for young viewers. Because while Superman may fight for the American way, he usually does so in a decidedly gentlemanly manner (he grew up in the Midwest, after all). Still, the PG-13-rated *Superman Returns* has its share of violent moments that can seem like so much visual krypton to a parent trying to limit a young child's exposure to images of fights, guns, and other assorted villainy.

Instead Try: *The Complete Superman Collection: Diamond Anniversary Edition.* Produced in the early 1940s, the seventeen classic Superman cartoons of Max and Dave Fleisher are still widely regarded as some of the finest work in animation history. With an art deco look and film noir feel, The Man of Steel's universe as rendered by the Fleishers is a sight to behold. And unlike more modern cartoons starring Clark Kent and his caped alter ego that go heavy on gratuitous violence (we're looking at you, *Superman Doomsday*), here the action is more than age-appropriate for the youngest of viewers.

SPIDERMAN

While some parents might remember the old web-slinger cartoon as being kid-friendly, the newer live-action Spiderman movies are much more adult in theme. There's Spidey's guilt over his uncle's death, there's Spidey's best friend's bloodthirst to kill the friendly neighborhood wall crawler, and there's, well, a whole bunch of violent action not suited for younger eyes.

Instead Try: The 1970s cartoon series, the one with the catchy "Spiderman, Spiderman. Does whatever a spider can" theme song.

THE X-MEN

One of the most popular and enduring comics in all of the superhero universes, the X-Men are best known now for their hit series of live action PG-13 movies.

While your active youngster may try to convince you that the onscreen violence perpetrated by Professor Charles Xavier and his band of mutants is not that much different than what can be found in many Saturday morning cartoons, you just aren't comfortable exposing your child to a character named Wolverine who defeats a mutant foe by kicking him in the crotch and delivering the line, "Grow those back."

Instead Try: *The Power Rangers.*

Like the X-Men, the Power Rangers fight crime with their superhuman strength, speed, and other abilities. But unlike The X-Men, the heroes and storylines of this long-running show (various seasons are available on DVD) were created for younger audiences. While there is some violence, it's cartoonish in nature. And one of The Power Rangers wears a pink costume. How rough can it get?

God is in the Tomato

This may not have happened to you, but we're going to ask anyway: Was there ever a time, back when you were a kid, when you flipped through the TV stations and stopped on a clay-animated series that looked kind of like Gumby? It was about a boy and his dog and, if you were in fact one of those people who accidentally stumbled on it, you watched for a while and then got a strange feeling that something wasn't quite right.

And then it happened. The G-word was mentioned.

The show we're referring to is *Davey and Goliath*. And the G stood for God—a word that doesn't appear much in mainstream children's programming.

Now, we're not going to say there should be more religious ideas in children's entertainment and we're not going to say there should be less. We're just saying it doesn't get talked about much. Except on the claymation boy-and-his-dog classic *Davey and Goliath*.

And more recently on the wacky, computer animated *Veggie Tales*. In the former, the message came rather overtly. In the latter, it comes from cucumbers and tomatoes. The difference between the two can be seen by considering an episode from each.

In the "On the Line" episode, Davey wants to show that you can talk to God even though God can't be seen with your eyes. So he makes a string telephone.

In "Gideon Tuba Warrior," Larry the Cucumber plays a version of the biblical Gideon, who is summoned by God to defeat an incoming pickle army and learns a little something about faith.

What can *Davey and Goliath* do that *Veggie Tales* can't? Make you cry your eyes out. Just try to watch the Easter episode in which Davey tries to cope with the death of his grandmother.

What can *Veggie Tales* do that *Davey and Goliath* can't? Rock. There's some terrific songwriting going on in the veggie bin, with such tunes as "We're The Pirates Who Don't Do Anything" and "The Credit Song" that transcend religious differences.

A Host of Changes (or, Wait, What Happened to the Other Guy?)

TV and Video

As in soap operas, there comes a time in some children's TV shows when an established actor needs to be replaced. This can be a delicate matter, given the passion with which kids can attach themselves to their favorite stars. (Come to think of it, it's probably even harder pulling off an actor switcharoo on soap opera actors, but that's another book.)

Here are a few prominent now-you-see-him/now-you-see-someone-else cases from recent entertainment history:

BLUE'S CLUES

Out: Steve Burns

Burns hosted the show from its inception in 1996 until hanging up his signature striped green rugby shirt in 2002 to pursue a music career (critical consensus on that: he's got surprising chops). In the Nickelodeon documentary *Behind the Clues,* Burns admitted there was a second factor motivating him to turn Blue's leash over to a new owner: "I didn't want to lose my hair in children's television," he said. We'll take that as a clue about his balding-early blues.

Controversy: What does Burns have in common with Paul McCartney

PART II: TV AND VIDEO ✻ 83

and Mikey, the kid from the Life cereal commercials? Far-reaching reports of their demise have been greatly exaggerated. In fact, after he left *Blue's Clues*, rumors that Burns had died of a drug overdose became so prevalent he made an appearance on *The Rosie O'Donnell Show* to set the record straight. Post B.C., music and acting became the focus. He played a flesh-eating vampire in the independent film *Neatherbeast Incorporated* and contributed a song to a They Might Be Giants tribute album. Who says there are no second acts?

In: Donovan Patton

Patton took the role of "Joe" – Blue's new owner–in 2002. Landing the gig wasn't easy. He beat out 1,500 other applicants and trained with Steve to get the new character just right. For starters, Joe wears different colored shirts and cargo pants instead of khakis. Good call, Joe. His hard work paid off. He earned a daytime Emmy nomination in 2005 for Outstanding Performer in a Children's Series. Then again, not a huge surprise as success runs in the Patton family. He is a cousin of General George Patton. No wonder he's able to keep Blue on such a tight leash.

Consensus: We miss ya Steve (and your hair, too.) But Joe's a swell guy. Old school episodes or brand new adventures with Blue, we're in good hands either way.

THE GOOD NIGHT SHOW

Out: Melanie Martinez

From 2005 to 2006, Martinez starred as the aptly named Melanie on this programming block for chips off the block. Known for her upbeat presentation of games, songs, and stories, Melanie was a hit with young kids and was likable to adults. To wit: when she left the show, thousands of parents contacted PBS about bringing her back.

Controversy: Martinez was fired in July 2006 when PBS discovered she had once acted in short films spoofing abstinence-only public service announcements. While sexual in nature, many—including Martinez—argued the films were fun satire and that she made the powers-that-be at PBS aware of them before she was hired as host. A backlash ensued. The *New York Times* weighed in, saying Martinez had become "a symbol of political expediency run amok." Even PBS's own ombudsman sided with her: "It would have been a greater bow to freedom of expression and against guilt by association for the program and PBS to stick by her." Post PBS, Martinez works as an actress. Among other things, she's done voice work for audio books and appeared as a panelist on VH-1. We miss you, Mel. Good night, and good luck.

In: Michele Lepe

As "Nina," the replacement *GNS* host, Michele Lepe made a smooth transition into the proceedings.

Until, that is, it was reported that—get this—she had once played a cop posing as a prostitute trying to catch johns in the oh-so-kid-friendly short film *Jamaica Hotel*. Sounds like a bunch of hypocritical P "BS" to us.

Consensus: Cover your eyes for a moment, moms, the rest of this section is for dads' eyes and dads' eyes only.

You're still reading.

Stop it.

Seriously, move on to the section about "The Wiggles" next. We need to talk to just your hubby for a sec . . .

Psst. Hey, dad. Look, just a little FYI: Nina sometimes does this little yoga routine, and the first time you see it you might feel kinda creepy about how it makes you feel because, well, in case you haven't noticed, Nina is totally smoking hot. It's ok, we felt a little creepy the first time we saw it, too. You know, given that she's hosting a kid's show and all. But like Vanessa Williams' yowza appearance in *Muppets from Space,* in time, you'll learn to enjoy it for what it is: a little gift for your enduring it all.

Now, go tell your wife we talked about . . . oh, say we told you an off-color joke about Fozzy Bear or something.

THE WIGGLES WORLD

Out: Greg Page

As one of the group's founding members and its lead singer, Greg Page was a (seemingly) indispensable part of The Wiggles (and its Playhouse Disney show *The Wiggles World*) until he retired from the group in 2006.

Controversy: Page quit the group in November 2006 when it was explained he had been diagnosed with a non-life-threatening disease called orthostatic intolerance, which causes a loss of balance when the sufferer stands up. Page had been largely absent from the *Wiggles* late shows in 2006, but the band remained mum on his mysterious absences until he officially left the group.

In: Sam Moran

As Page's understudy for nine years, Moran was already well-versed in the Wiggly ways when he was asked to don the yellow shirt and front the group full-time. The reaction: sort of Menudo-esque. One of the reasons for continuing, after all, was the knowledge that a good chunk of their core audience wouldn't even recognize the change. Ouch!

Consensus: Which one is which again? Doesn't matter. Kids like whoever's got the yellow shirt on. Feel better, Greg. And Greg . . . oops, we mean Sam, enjoy your time in the not-particularly-face-recognizing spotlight.

Ten Children's TV Shows To Know That We Couldn't Fit In Anywhere Else

1 *Howdy Doody.* You don't remember the popular 1950s puppet program *Howdy Doody.* Your parents probably don't even remember *Howdy Doody.* But we bring it up here because it is an oft-referenced cultural landmark. There. We've mentioned it. Let's move on.

2 *The Electric Company.* Flush from the success of *Sesame Street,* the powers that be at PBS went looking for a show that could be the kid equivalent of a doctorate program for those youngsters who had earned their Sesame masters. The result was this slightly-longer-attention-span show featuring a now-familiar cast including Rita Moreno and Morgan Freeman

offering wacky sketches to encourage reading comprehension. Back in the pre-home video, pre-home computer, and pre-hundreds of channels days, you could actually get kids to willingly watch a show about reading comprehension. It ran for six seasons and clocked in over 750 episodes.

3 *H.R. Pufnstuf.* For a while there in the early 1970s, Saturday morning TV looked like a clubhouse for unwanted mascots. That's thanks to the brother-brother team of Sid and Marty Krofft, who created series after series featuring actors in oversized costumes with minimal facial movement. While *Sigmund and the Sea Monsters, Lidsville,*

TV and Video

and *The Bugaloos* have their fans, we prefer their flagship series, *H.R. Pufnstuf*, named for the dinosaurish mayor of Living Island. Our hero, Jimmy (played by the same kid who played the Artful Dodger in the movie musical *Oliver!*) and a talking flute (don't ask) are cast ashore there, where Puf and his friends (including, inexplicably, a Judy Garlandesque frog) are in a turf war with Witchiepoo, who flies around on the Vroom Broom. When the kids are asleep, check out the DVD of the HBO series *Mr. Show*, which featured a hilarious parody called *The Altered State of Druggachusetts*. The odd thing: it's not that different from the original.

4 *Land of the Lost.* When Marshall, Will, and Holly—on a routine expedition—met the greatest earthquake ever known (or so the show's theme song tells us anyway), they found themselves in a prehistoric land populated with dinosaurs, lizardlike creatures called Sleestak,

an Ewok-meets-caveman little fella named Cha-ka, and the worst production values in the history of Saturday morning television. While this 1970s Sid and Marty Krofft series (available on DVD) has become something of a cult classic with older viewers, it's likely to go one of two ways with your little one. The stilted acting and awful stop-motion animation techniques are something so totally different to junior's regular rotation of shows that it may capture his imagination. Or, more likely, he'll ask you to put on something an actual computer was used to help create.

5 *Zoom.* This PBS series aired in the 1970s and was revived from 1999–2005. We're guessing it will be back again at some point, so we're including it here. In case you missed one of the *Zoom* periods, the show's premise was simple: kids you wish you were hanging out with rather than watching TV created crafts, performed science

experiments, played games, and told jokes. And viewers were encouraged to send in their own ideas, which were read on the air (which is why an entire generation or two knows that the zip code for Boston, Massachusetts is 0-2-1-3-4).

6 *The Magic School Bus.* While we were big fans of *The Magic School Bus* when it took its first television ride in 1994, in hindsight, we're not so sure. Oh, it's great that kids were learning all about photosynthesis and other scientific stuff (and cool that, for once, a woman was in the Mr. Wizardish role), but for pre-K kids, the show may give them a really false idea of what grade school is going to be like. I mean, what teacher can compete with Lily Tomlin's Miss Frizzle for coolness? And what happens when your kid realizes that her school bus can't enter the human body or visit outer space?

7 *Fat Albert and the Cosby Kids.* Just the fact that the word *fat* appears in the title of this cartoon—and that the character in question is, indeed, morbidly obese—tells you that this landmark show was the product of a different era. And thank goodness for that. Because this 1970s Bill Cosby creation—about a group of kids living and learning in a not exactly affluent inner city neighborhood—could never have happened today. Someone would make the case that Mushmouth was incomprehensible (that's the point!), that you couldn't call a character Dumb Donald, and that Fat Albert should demonstrate proper eating habits.

8 *Full House.* Once upon a time, *Full House* was a bland and critically panned sitcom about a San Francisco widower raising three daughters with the help of his Elvis-loving brother-in-law and his Bullwinkle-obsessed best friend. Aside from the fact that it introduced the world to Mary Kate and

Ashley Olsen, there was nothing particularly memorable about the series when it was abruptly cancelled after a remarkable eight-season run. Until, that is, it began airing in syndication years later. Oddly, in the post-*Seinfeld*, post-modern world of the twenty-first century, *Full House,* with its goofy yet endearing family values, found a whole new generation of viewers who don't find it bland at all. In fact, they find it kind of refreshing.

9 *The Brady Bunch.* It's the story of a lovely lady who was living with three very lovely girls. Then all of a sudden she meets this architect—a man named Brady—and as fate would have it, he was living with three boys of his own. In fact, he was their father. Thank God. Wouldn't it have been creepy if he wasn't? Anyway this bunch of folks somehow formed a family, hired a housekeeper to help out, and intentional and unintentional hilarity ensued in syndication ever since. And it still holds up, for some totally inexplicable reason.

10 *Mr. Rogers' Neighborhood.* Often parodied, never duplicated. We would be remiss if we didn't include a shout out to the sweatered one, the man who gently guided generations. While his influence has diminished over the years—when you are irreplaceable, you tend not to be replaced—he remains the dad that the rest of us papas all wish we could be.

Intermezzo: Oh, the Places Dr. Seuss Has Gone

Theodore "Dr. Seuss" Geisel revolutionized the way kids—and parents—read books. He created indelible characters and exquisitely silly rhymes. And while he was alive, his control of his creations was unprecedented.

And then, well, he died. Which, we know, happens. But when it happened to Dr. Seuss, things changed.

Here's a timeline to help reintroduce you to the great one. Be aware, though, that in the interest of brevity, it skips over many major works and lots of minor ones. (The guy wrote and illustrated forty-four books.)

1926: Theodore Geisel, who used the pen name "Seuss" at Dartmouth, adds "Dr." to his moniker.

1937: Dr. Seuss's first children's book, *And to Think I Saw It on Mulberry Street*, is published. It still holds up.

1940: *Horton Hatches the Egg* is published. Frankly, we like Horton more than the more popular *Cat in the Hat*. He doesn't make us as nervous. And he doesn't teach lessons of peace and tolerance—he *embodies* peace and tolerance.

1947: *McElligot's Pool* is published. "If a fellow is patient," says the narrator, "he might get his wish." The cool word there is *might*. Unlike many other children's book writers, Seuss doesn't promise easy answers.

1951: Seuss's cartoon short, *Gerald McBoing-Boing*, which tells the story of a kid who only talks in sound effects, wins an Academy Award. It represents Seuss's understanding that some stories are meant for some media and some for others. Of course, after Seuss's death it becomes a book, a board book, a board game . . . (but we're getting ahead of ourselves).

1953: The Seuss-written fantasy feature film *The 5,000 Fingers of Dr. T* is released. It's a bit of a head-trip, with the feel of the kind of thing Tim Burton would make forty years later. And while the look and feel is definitely Seussian, the doc himself wasn't happy with it.

1954: *Horton Hears a Who* is published. By the time you read this, the long-suffering elephant's adventures trying to protect the tiny residents of Whoville will be the subject of a major motion picture. You already know whether or not it worked. We're not going to guess. We're just glad it wasn't live action.

1957: *How the Grinch Stole Christmas* and *The Cat in the Hat* are both published, perhaps the strongest single-year doubleheader in the history of literature. The latter was written on a bet that Seuss couldn't write a children's reader with the 225 basic sight-list words used in most primers. The goal was to figure out a way to encourage young kids to read (prior to Seuss, the main readers were the dull, dull, dull Dick and Jane books).

1958: Dr. Seuss takes over as president of Beginner Books, which was launched with *The Cat in the Hat*. *Yertle the Turtle* and *The Cat in the Hat Comes Back* are published.

1960: *Green Eggs and Ham* is published. Breakfast hasn't been the same since.

1966: An animated version of *How the Grinch Stole Christmas* premiers on television, directed by Chuck Jones, best known for his classic Bugs Bunny cartoons. The quality control—from the Boris Karloff narration through the Albert Hague score (trivia note: Hague played music teacher Shorofsky in the movie and TV series *Fame*)—is evident throughout. In short, a masterpiece.

1968: *Hop on Pop* is published, causing generations of dads to suffer bellyaches from bouncing kids.

1971: An animated take on *The Cat in the Hat* premiers on television, with song parodist Allan Sherman as the voice of the troublemaking feline. *The Lorax* is published.

1984: *The Butter Battle Book* is published. Dr. Seuss wins the Pulitzer Prize. Adults are starting to realize that there are some serious messages behind some of the Seuss books.

1990: *Oh the Places You'll Go* is published and becomes a best-seller thanks in large part to the fact that it provides an easy out for valedictorians trying to come up with graduation speeches. But be warned: your young 'un will probably say "Go, already," if you try to read him the whole thing.

1991: Dr. Seuss dies. Soon thereafter, all licensing hell breaks lose. You see, while Seuss was alive, the doc was ultracareful in how his characters were handled. Which is why you didn't see a whole lot of Seussian toothbrushes pre-1991. But after his death, his widow caved. Defenders say her change of strategy was to fight all of the bootleg products hitting the market. And because if she didn't do anything with the characters, they would eventually enter the public domain.

Okay, maybe. But Seuss's words and pictures have now been cut, rearranged, and watered down in so many ways that it's difficult for a new parent to know the knockoffs from the originals. In addition, the good Seuss name was attached to 1994's *In Search of Dr. Seuss* (call us Grinches, but we'll take the originals over this "all-star" tribute biography with Matt Frewer as the Cat in the Hat) and the 1996 Nickelodeon series *The Wubbulous World of Dr. Seuss,* created by Jim Henson and company (who forgot to add wit into the mix). And then there was . . .

2000: *How the Grinch Stole Christmas,* a big box-office hit, despite the fact that it's creepier than it is funny. Do your kids a favor and stick to the animated classic. Of course, this Grinch looks like *Citizen Kane* compared to *The Cat in the Hat* film, but we'll get to that momentarily.

That same year, *Seussical the Musical* premiers on Broadway. Initial critical reaction is not good to the show that attempts to combine the plots of many Seuss classics. But the show has proven very popular in regional theaters (after being rewritten post-Broadway by the creative team). Horton, by the way, gets the best songs. It's worth checking out if your kid isn't likely to be freaked out by the Wickersham Brothers.

In other 2000 Seuss news, *Publishers Weekly*'s list of the top-selling children's books of all time lists six of the doc's books in the top 20.

2003: The feature film version of *Dr. Seuss's The Cat in the Hat,* starring Mike Myers, is the low point in Seuss cash-ins. Critic Charles Taylor at salon.com wisely noted that it offered "the best argument yet made for extending artists' rights beyond the grave."

2006: Dr. Seuss's *How the Grinch Stole Christmas* opens on Broadway for a limited run, returned for the 2007 holiday season, and promises to be a perennial New York staple. It includes songs from the animated special as well as new tunes.

2008: A computer-animated version of *Horton Hears a Who*, from the folks behind *Ice Age*, is released in theaters. It's ok.

Part III

MUSIC

We were going to suggest in this introduction that there really is no reason for there to be a separation between kids' music and adult music. After all, isn't it all, well, music? But then we got to thinking. And our thinking led us to two simple facts:

Fact 1: No adult can tolerate the Doodlebops.

Fact 2: No child can tolerate Philip Glass.

And once we established that difference, we were off and running. In the following section, you'll learn about children's entertainers, children's music, adult music that sounds like kid's music, and much more.

Why It's Okay for You to Hate Children's Entertainers

1. One of the features that characterize successful and effective children's entertainers is their commitment and focus. They grasp–whether intuitively or through intense work–how to satisfy the needs of a very fickle and distractible audience. It is these same features that make some of the best children's entertainers very scary to adults. Why are we so creeped out by them? In part, because the Raffis of the world, the Tom Chapins, the Sharons, Loises and Brams, and the Trout Fishing in Americas, are doing what we often can't do–sing, dance, and get our kids to sit still and pay attention.

2. No matter how good a children's musician may be, you can't help but think that, if they didn't have something wrong with them, they would be playing for adults. As such, they are the dentists of the entertainment business.

3. They smile. A lot. If anyone at your office smiled half as much as your average children's entertainer, you'd steer clear of his or her cubicle.

The Six Classes of Kids' Musicians

Before we go ahead and classify, let's talk for a second about Frank Sinatra and the Beatles:

Sinatra didn't write his own songs.

The Beatles, for the most part, did.

That doesn't make one greater than the other.

So we're not going to say that the best kids' entertainers write their own songs. We are going to separate these folks into groups, to help with your understanding of what you are going to be trapped listening to for the next decade or so.

A Real band playing their own music and instruments (i.e. Trout Fishing in America)

B Real band playing classics and covers (i.e. the guy trying to get the four-year-olds at a birthday party to sing along to "Who Let the Dogs Out?")

C Prefab band created for television who play their own instruments (i.e. The Imagination Movers)

D Prefab band created for television that includes puppets (i.e. Johnny and the Sprites)

E Prefab band created for television that includes a hip hop singer/ train conductor and a beat boxer/railroad engineer (i.e. Choo Choo Soul)

F The Doodlebops

What you do with this information is up to you.

Our Favorite Performances of Children's Songs by Famous Entertainers

You don't have to limit yourself to children's singers in order to hear kid music. Just as most grown-up musicians eventually take a run at a holiday music album, most also attempt at least one children's song. The results aren't always winners. But here's some that are:

Song: "Teddy Bear's Picnic"
Artists: David Grisman and Jerry Garcia
Kinda reminds you of: The mellower stuff on The Grateful Dead's *Reckoning* album.
Why parents will like it: When the erstwhile Dead guitarist rocks his signature chromatic stylings on the ol' acoustic, it kind of makes you want to hold up a lighter or something.
Why kids will like it: Teddy bears partying in the woods with just a small, ominous hint that this ain't gonna be no fancy tea-and-biscuits affair ("if you go out in the woods today, you'd better not go alone")—why would children not like grooving to this folk classic?
Find it on: iTunes or the CD *Not for Kids Only*

* * *

Song: "Wynken and Blynken and Nod"
Artist: The Doobie Brothers
Kinda reminds you of: "Old Black Water"

Why parents will like it: Michael McDonald on lead vocals singing about three fishermen in a wooden shoe. C'mon, does it get any better than this?

Why kids will like it: An introduction to subtext. "Wait a second, mom, you mean all along this whole thing was a metaphor for bedtime? Wynken and Blynken are really two little eyes and Nod, a little head? That would make their wooden shoe, like, what . . . a bed?! Start that Ivy League fund stat!"

Find it on: iTunes or the CD *Long Train Runnin' 1970–2000*

✳ ✳ ✳

Song: **"Lizard Lips and Chicken Hips"**

Artist: Bruce Springsteen

Kinda of reminds you of: "Red Headed Woman"

Why parents will like it: It's got all the good stuff when the Boss straps on an acoustic and a harmonica minus all the usual angsty social and/or political commentary.

Why kids will like it: A tale about mom making a meal out of weird crap like rabbit ears and camel rears. Sweet!

Find it on: the CD *For Our Children: 10th Anniversary Edition*

✳ ✳ ✳

Song: **"Three is a Magic Number"**

Artist: Blind Melon

Kinda reminds you of: "Schoolhouse Rock" with better guitars, louder amps, and a superior drummer.

Why parents like it: Takes you back to your youth (assuming your youth included "Schoolhouse Rock") with a funky new twist.

Why kids will like it: You mean learning about math is cool? Cool!

Find it on: iTunes or the CD *The Best of Blind Melon*

✳ ✳ ✳

Song: **"I Wanna Be Like You"**

Artist: Big Bad Voodoo Daddy

Kinda reminds you of: That one year in the late 1990s when this

kind of music was everywhere and for one brief, glorious moment, Brian Setzer was employable again.
Why parents like it: It jumps, jives, and wails.
Why kids will like it: "Hey, it's that song from *The Jungle Book!* Only it's got loud horns!"
Find it on: iTunes or the soundtrack to the movie *Swingers*

✳ ✳ ✳

Song: "**I Don't Want to Live on the Moon**"
Artist: Shawn Colvin and Ernie
Kinda sounds like: "Sunny Came Home"
Why parents like it: In the hands of Colvin and her ethereal vocals, you realize what a lovely song this really is. And when Ernie kicks in on harmonies, it's like it was written this way.
Why kids like it: Duh. It's a song about visiting space and dinosaurs and the sea.
Find it on: iTunes or the CD *Elmopalooza*

✳ ✳ ✳

Song: "**We're Gonna Be Friends**"
Artist: The White Stripes
Kinda sounds like: The song on the opening credits of *Napoleon Dynamite*. Oh, wait. That's because it is.
Why parents like it: Because while those other, poor, sad, foolish, new parents are driving around with, like, lullabies and crap in their CD changers, you can say you're still jamming to The White Stripes!
Why kids like it: They recognize it from advertisements for *Sesame Street*.
Find it on: iTunes or the CD *White Blood Cells*

✳ ✳ ✳

Song: "**The Rainbow Connection**"
Artist: Willie Nelson
Kinda sounds like: "Always On My Mind"
Why parents will like it: A spare, unique interpretation with some unusual-but-memorable vocal

cadences and classic Willie guitar solo chops.

Why kids will like it: Rainbows are beautiful and so is this song.

Find it on: iTunes or the CD *Rainbow Connection*

* * *

Song: "Just Happy to Be Me"
Artist: Fugees
Kinda sounds like: "Killing Me Softly With His Song"
Why parents will like it: There has never been a cooler way to learn the alphabet in the history of methods that teach learning about the alphabet.
Why kids will like it: Ditto.
Find it on: iTunes or the CD *Elmopalooza*

* * *

Song: "My Flying Saucer"
Artist: Billy Bragg and Wilco
Kinda sounds like: The jammin' tunes on *Yankee Hotel Foxtrot*
Why parents will like it: Because it rocks!
Why kids will like it: Because it's

about a flying saucer!
Find it on: iTunes or the CD *Mermaid Avenue Vol 2*

* * *

Song: "John Lee Supertaster"
Artist: They Might Be Giants
Kinda sounds like: They Might Be Giants
Why parents will like it: Finally a superhero with powers dads in particular can truly relate to.
Why kids will like it: From the prologue to the last note, the whole thing is damn funny.
Find it on: iTunes or the CD *No!*

* * *

Song: "Somewhere Over the Rainbow"
Artist: Israel Kamakawiwo'ole
Kinda sounds like: The music from a credit card commercial (but in a good way).
Why parents will like it: Mommies and daddies always appreciate a guy who can rock the ukulele to great artistic effect. It's one of the rules.

Music

Why kids will like it: "Oh, it's the song from *Wizard of Oz* but without all the vocal histrionics. Nice."
Find it on: iTunes or the CD *Alone in IZ world.*

✳ ✳ ✳

Song: **"Mary Had a Little Lamb"**
Artist: Stevie Ray Vaughn and Double Trouble
Kinda sounds like: *Texas Flood*
Why parents will like it: SRV knows his way around a fret board.
Why kids will like it: It's a funky version of a song they already know the lyrics to.
Find it on: iTunes or the CD *Texas Flood*

✳ ✳ ✳

Song: **"Bibbidi-Bobbidi-Boo"**
Artist: Louis Armstrong
Kinda sounds like: "Fantastic, That's You"
Why parents will like it: Because you have to smile when Satchmo sings.
Why kids will like it: Because they'll think Grover is singing.

Find it on: *Disney Songs the Satchmo Way.*

✳ ✳ ✳

Song: **"Who's Afraid of the Big Bad Wolf?"**
Artist: L.L. Cool J
Kinda sounds like: A song session in pre-juvie.
Why parents will like it: Hearing L.L. sing about "handsome piggy-wigs"
Why kids will like it: Because L.L. takes the creative leap of making himself the third pig—and has some serious ideas about what he'll do to the wolf.
Find it on: *Simply Mad About the Mouse.* (What good luck: The disc also contains a rollicking Gypsy Kings version of "I've Got No Strings" and Ric Ocasek having fun with "Zip-A-Dee-Doo-Dah."
What bad luck: It also has Michael Bolton doing "A Dream is a Wish Your Heart Makes."

Great Adult Songs that Could Easily Be Passed Off As Children's Songs

Every once in a while, a song enters the popular adult consciousness that could just as easily be a kids song. Play these songs again in your mental iPod and ask yourself: who are they really written for? We think the answer to that question is: people under four feet tall. And we don't mean the guy from "Willow."

"Yellow Submarine" by the Beatles

"Good Morning Starshine" from the original cast album of *Hair*

"Do You Believe in Magic?" by The Lovin' Spoonful

"Walking on Sunshine" by Katrina and the Waves

"Daydream Believer" by The Monkees

"Put a Smile on Your Face" by Coldplay

"The Circle Game" by Joni Mitchell

"Don't Worry Be Happy" by Bobby McFerrin

"Shower The People" by James Taylor

"The Tin Man" by America

"Happiness Runs" by Donovan

"Feeling Groovy" by Simon and Garfunkle

Music Quiz: The Songs Remain the Same

You'll never know the songwriters behind these tunes. But they will be burned into your consciousness soon (if they aren't already). To see how far gone you already are, take this musical quiz:

1. You probably know that "the wheels on the bus go round and round." But how do the people on the bus go?
a) Back and forth
b) To and fro
c) Up and down
d) Front and back

2. "Row, Row, Row Your Boat" is often performed in this type of musical style in which two or more voices begin singing at different times.
a) A circle
b) A sphere
c) An oval
d) A round

3. If you put salicadoola together with menchicaboola what have you got? _____.

4. What animal chases what other animal around a mulberry bush?

5. What do you NOT do "if you're happy and you know it?"
a) Clap your hands
b) Jump for joy
c) Shout "Hurray!"
d) Stomp your feet

6. I'm a little teapot. What is my

stature?

a) Short and stout

b) Long and tall

c) Wee and fat

d) Small and free

7. In "The Song That Never Ends" (aka "The Song That Doesn't End") what is the last word sung before the song repeats?

a) Belly

b) Because

c) Big

d) Bends

8. True or False: "Happy Birthday to You" is the most popular song in the English language.

9. What did the itsy bitsy spider do after it was washed away by the rain?

a) Climb up the spout again

b) Run away

c) Spin a web

d) File a complaint

10. "The Alphabet Song" has the exact same melody as this iconic children's song_____ and this nursery rhyme _____.

11. In "The Farmer in the Dell" the farmer takes a wife and the wife takes a child. What does the child take?

a) A cow

b) A rat

c) Some cheese

d) A nurse

12. In "She'll be Comin' 'Round the Mountain" how many horses will the "she" in question be driving?

13. Complete the lyric from this never-ending song: "Whenever we go out/The people always shout _____."

14. True or False: "When You Wish Upon A Star" is featured in the movie *Cinderella*.

15. According to the teacher in "Mary Had a Little Lamb," why does the lamb love Mary so?

But Isn't It Really About, You Know, Drugs? The Definitive Dope on "Puff the Magic Dragon"

When Sigmund Freud was asked about his fixation with cigars (one of the most phallic of all symbols) and what it represented, the good doctor famously replied, "Sometimes a cigar is just a cigar." In other words, when you're looking for a deep meaning in a symbol, perhaps you need look no further than its surface.

By Freud's logic, sometimes a puff is just a puff. Or is it?

That's the debate that has surrounded a different kind of "Puff"—the protagonist of Peter, Paul and Mary's folk classic "Puff the Magic Dragon"—since the song was first released in 1962. To set up this long-standing controversy, we now take you to a scene from the movie *Meet the Parents*.

[Robert De Niro (Jack Bynes) and Ben Stiller (Greg Focker) driving in a car listening to "Puff the Magic Dragon"]

Greg Focker: Who'd have thought it wasn't about a dragon.

Jack Byrnes: Huh?

To be fair, from the Byrds' "8 Miles High" to the Beatles' "Lucy in the Sky with Diamonds," cynics, moralists, and conspiracy theorists have claimed that there's more to these songs and others than initially meets the ear. Perhaps. But when the Byrds and the Beatles play coy about their songs' meanings, that's one thing. They are songs written by rock stars for adult and adolescent fans of rock music.

But what about "Puff the Magic Dragon," one of the most beloved songs for kids of all ages? Is it a positive, if melancholy, anthem about childhood imagination or a subliminal call to action to "just say yes"?

The story behind the creation of the song goes something like this: a nineteen-year-old college student named Leonard Lipton was inspired by the Ogden Nash poem "Custard the Dragon" to pen his own ode to fire-breathing beasts. He showed his rhymes to his buddy and fellow Cornell student Peter Yarrow who promptly added music and additional lyrics to it, transforming Lipton's words into what would become one of the most beloved tunes of all time.

A couple years later, Yarrow would form a band called Peter, Paul and Mary, and "Puff" would soon become one of their signature songs (reaching number two on the Billboard charts).

So what's all the fuss about?

Intentional or not, for those looking, the song can be read as being filled with not-so-subtle references to the marijuana and drug cultures. From the obvious "puff" reference to young friend Jackie Paper (can't puff without paper) to the song's fantasyland setting of Honalee (read by some as a reference to Hanalei, Hawaii, which is known for its marijuana production) to a whole bunch of other if-you-want-to-see-it-it's-there drug references (i.e. "sealing wax," the haze of frolicking in the "autumn mist," etc.).

Peter Yarrow, for one, has maintained that the only kind of magic he intended for his famous dragon was simply the kind that comes with being around child-hood innocence. "As the principal writer of the song, I can assure it's a song about innocence lost. It's easier to interpret the 'Star Spangle Banner' as a drug song than 'Puff the Magic Dragon' . . . When Puff was written, I was too innocent to know about drugs. What kind of a mean-spirited SOB would write a children's song with a covert drug message?"

Wherever you come down on this debate, one thing remains pretty certain: Whatever it's about, "Puff the Magic Dragon" is a pretty great and timeless song.

And we're not just blowing smoke.

A Wiggly Primer for the Uninitiated Parent

Hello New Parents!!!
Are you ready to rock?!
Are you ready to roll?!
Are you ready to Wiggle?!

What do you mean you have "no idea what that means?"

You know, The Wiggles. Greg, Anthony, Murray, Jeff, and Sam.

No?

OK, let's back up. In case you're not yet tuned in to the Down Under's Fabbest Foursome (which pretty much means your child has yet to enter the 2-to-8 demographic) let's get you caught up quickly so you know what you'll be getting yourself into and soon.

The Wiggles are a wildly successful, umm . . . that is, they're really good at . . . The Wiggles routinely earn millions of dollars each year, making them Australia's most lucrative entertainers, often outearning Nicole Kidman and AC/DC's annual takes combined. Clearly, they're good at something. After all, they've got their own Disney Channel show—not to mention the dozens of CDs, DVDs, books, cars, dolls, and fake instruments bearing their likenesses.

The most initiated parents can easily explain the enduring appeal of the Wiggles. So here goes: the Wiggles are popular with both the toddler set and their moms because . . . well? Let's try to sort this all out.

There is no hard, formal evidence of what we're about to suggest, but it feels true enough to present it as if it's a fact anyway: most men hate the Wiggles. They find them unnerving in much the same way that they find it unnerving to learn that their toddler sons have taken to playing with Bratz dolls and tea sets. For many fathers, their childrens' interest in the Wiggles is a phase that must be tolerated until their kids move on to worshiping more acceptable heroes. Like Barry Bonds.

Women, on the other hand, seem to love these guys. According to an article in Australia's *Sun Herald* titled, "Women Go Wild for Wiggles," many moms are apparently more than simply fans of what these blokes are teaching their children: "Desperate housewives in the U.S. have besieged the Wiggles with sexually suggestive letters and comments, including explicit references about band members including Anthony Field (the blue Wiggle) and Murray Clark (the red Wiggle)."

So women love the Wiggles, and men hate them. Why? Could it be that it's because the Wiggles are exposing some very real truths about masculinity that divide their adult audience along gender lines? Certainly seems reasonable.

Maybe the best way to tease that one out is to take a look at what, exactly, the Wiggles are all about.

Music

Most children's programming has a message it wants to get across to its target audience. Mister Rogers, you will recall, wanted all of his viewers to know how "special" they were. *Blue's Clues* concerns itself with celebrating intellectual curiosity.

You might ask yourself, then, what message is it that the Wiggles are trying to articulate?

Like the Teletubbies before them, each one of the Wiggles has an identifiable color. Greg (and now Sam, his replacement) wears yellow. Anthony, blue. Murray's got the red shirt. And Jeff is Mr. Purple. And, like the Teletubbies before them, each one of the Wiggles also has a defining shorthand personality/hobby. Jeff, for instance, likes to sleep a lot. Anthony is known for having an insatiable appetite. In other words, his talent is that he likes to eat. Murray plays guitar (the three-chord strumming kind, not the Jeff Beck kind). Finally, since he's the only one who ever gets to drive the "Big Red Car" on

screen, Greg/Sam is known as the group's above-average driver (on stage Greg's defining characteristic was that he was the group's most prodigious belly sweater.)

The Wiggles live in the Wiggle's World–a kind of H.R. Pufnstuf-meets-Roald Dahl backdrop with their friends Wags the Dog, Henry the Octopus, Dorothy the Dinosaur, and perhaps their best friend of all, Captain Feathersword, the friendly pirate.

The primary function of the Wiggles World is to provide a rubric to glue together a bunch of song-and-dance numbers. The odd thing, though, is that these songs really aren't about anything, nor do they really have much of a pedagogical component. In many instances, they are nothing more than a bunch of self-reflexive songs about the Wiggles themselves and what the Wiggles themselves do best, which is this: absolutely nothing.

Case in point: the jury is still out on the Wiggles' level of instrumental talent–especially when they perform live. The explanation to this very issue in the FAQ section of their website is extremely cagey.

When you put all of this together–the Wiggles' ridiculously underwhelming defining characteristics, their meaningless, lessonless lyrics, their dubious musical talent–what the Wiggles are about almost seems to present itself in large neon lights that say this: "It's okay if you and your stupid life turn out to be mediocre. Look at us!"

At first blush, it might not seem like that's exactly the most awe-inspiring lesson. But when you think about it, given the reality and inevitability of it for most of us, one could argue that it's perhaps the *most* important lesson our kids can be learning upfront.

Boiled down to their essences, songs like "Wiggle Party" and "Get Ready to Wiggle" and "In the Wiggle's World" are tunes that are more or less saying this: "Chances are, like us, the long road to medi-ocrity is probably one you're headed down, too. Wanna dance?"

How to Tell the Beatles from the Wiggles

Defining Characteristics

Beatles: John ("the clever one"); Paul ("the cute one"); George ("the quiet one"); Ringo ("the funny one")

Wiggles: Greg/Sam ("the yellow one"); Anthony ("the blue one"); Murray ("the red one"); Jeff ("the purple one")

Preferred Method of Transportation

Beatles: A Yellow Submarine

Wiggles: The Big Red Car

Best Song About an Octopus

Beatles: "Octopus's Garden"

Wiggles: "Henry the Octopus"

Once opened a concert for

Beatles: Billy Shears

Wiggles: Barney

Early band incarnation featuring at least two members of the group

Beatles: The Quarrymen

Wiggles: The Cockroaches

Lead guitarist's reaction to former band leader's personal tragedy

Beatles: "As far as I'm concerned, there won't be a Beatles reunion as long as John Lennon remains dead." –George Harrison on his longtime friend and band mate

Wiggles: "Children tend to center on one thing, so if he's wearing the yellow skivvy, he's got black hair–he's pretty much Greg."– Murray Clark on replacement lead singer Sam Moran stepping in for the retiring-due-to-health-issues Greg Page.

Band member who left the group just before the big fame and money kicked in
The Beatles: Pete Best
The Wiggles: Philip Wilcher

If for some reason you find yourself high on an illegal psychotropic substance, put on
Beatles: "Tomorrow Never Knows," "Within You or Without You," the White Album
Wiggles: "Rainbow of Colors," "Take a Trip Out on the Sea," "Cold Spaghetti Western"

Weird band rumor or superstition
The Beatles: Paul is dead.
The Wiggles: For several years they traveled in two separate buses and planes so if a disaster occurred, half the group would survive.

First film
The Beatles: *A Hard Day's Night.* Currently ranked the fourth greatest film of all time on Rotten Tomatoes.

The Wiggles: *The Wiggles Movie.* The fifth highest grossing movie in Australia in 1998.

"5th member" candidates
Beatles: George Martin; Brian Epstein; Stuart Sutcliff; Billy Preston; Pete Best
Wiggles: Captain Fethersword; Dorothy the Dinosaur; Wags the Dog; Henry the Octopus; Paul Field

Gal-pal who always seems to bring the group down
Beatles: Yoko One
Wiggles: Officer Beaples

Nice shout-out to noncarnivores message
Beatles: Paul's vegetarian activism.
Wiggles: "Fruit Salad . . .Yummy, Yummy"

When *You* Need a Good Cry

Satellite radio doesn't yet have a channel for it, but if it did, there would be plenty of songs to fill up a station that focuses on nothing but Songs Designed to Make Parents Cry. For some, these are cathartic. For others, they are shameless. Either way, get out your handkerchiefs. Here we go:

"Butterfly Kisses"—in which Tim McGraw listens to his daughter as she prays, takes his girl on her first pony ride, deals with her botched attempt to make a cake, survives her sweet-sixteen, and then marries her off, picking up eyelid smooches along the life-cycley way.

"Cat's in the Cradle"—in which the narrator doesn't pay much attention to his kid because there are, you know, planes to catch and bills to pay. Karma bites him back when his kid grows up and doesn't have time for him (although, to give junior some credit, he does say "please" when asking for the car keys).

"Daddy's Little Girl"—in which legendary vocalist Al Martino references a gem, a star, sugar, spice, a rainbow, a pot of gold, a treasure, the Easter bunny, Christmas, and a holy and beautiful light in telling fathers-of-the-bride everywhere how incredibly wonderful their just-wed daughters are. Every time you hear it at a wedding from now on, you'll be rendered helpless.

"Father and Son"—in which the titular old but happy pop and anguished offspring voice off against each other's ignorance, leading junior to declare that he has to go away. I'll never be like that with my son, you'll insist. Okay. Believe that.

"Gracie" by Ben Folds—in which Ben Folds realizes that "life flies by in seconds" and that he's got to hang onto the feeling of numbness when his kid falls asleep on his arm. Teen fans might think it's cute. You'll be devastated.

"Holes in the Floor of Heaven"— in which Colin Raye has to explain to his daughter that that ain't a rainstorm, it's her dead mama's tears. Gotta love country music.

"Ready Set Don't Go"— in which Billy Ray Cyrus tries to be strong while his daughter takes off from "the startin' line of the rest of her life." Nice that daughter Miley has a bigger career than pop's.

Why *Schoolhouse Rock* Still Rocks

Chances are, if you're a parent who grew up in the early 1970s to mid-1980s, you share a very specific bond with other parents who came of age in this era.

Specifically, you recognize that of all the digits in the mathematical universe, one in particular is the most special. (Hello? It's three, and that's a magic number.) You know, without hesitation, the essential function of "conjunction junction." (Duh. Hooking up words and phrases and clauses.) But mostly, above all else, you're something of an unofficial expert on what it takes for a bill to become a law (in addition to a bunch of political red tape, there's lot of hoping, praying, and bantering with a wide-eyed boy.)

Yes, if you know all of these things, you've likely seen or heard your fair share of *Schoolhouse Rock*. But if for some reason you've missed out—or if you need a refresher course—we're here to get you in tune.

In the early 1970s, an advertising executive named David McCall observed that his son knew the words to just about every rock song on the radio. But when it came to memorizing multiplication tables, his memory wasn't nearly as acute.

Thus, an idea (and a coming-of-age soundtrack) was born: what would happen if lively music and animation was married to traditional lessons about grammar, history, multiplication, science, government, and finance?

The result? *Schoolhouse Rock*, an Emmy Award–winning series of three-minute education vignettes combining animation and music that aired on ABC from 1972 to 1985.

How did this experiment stand head and shoulders above a litany of lousy "hey, kids, check out this funky multiplication rap, yo" pretenders that have tried and failed to capture *SHR*'s essential greatness?

For starters—and this is especially important to newish parents who are beginning to realize they are no longer the CEO of their car's CD player—the music is really good.

Scratch that. It's great.

The *rock* in *Schoolhouse Rock* is something of a misnomer as only a few of *SHR*'s songs can be classified as true "rock" songs (i.e. "Elementary, My Dear") the rest are jazz, blues, pop, and whatever the heck the genre "Lolly, Lolly, Lolly, Get Your Adverbs Here" falls into. (Our best guess? "Neo-barbershop.")

As but one example of the quality of the artistry behind *SHR* music, one need look no further than its very first song—the aforementioned "Three is a Magic

Number," composed by Bob Dorough. Before his many *SHR* contributions, Dorough was a celebrated jazz pianist known for collaborations with Miles Davis and penning a Grammy-nominated song for Mel Torme. As another example, check out the Dorough song "Figure Eight"—a beautiful if melancholy tune from which instrumental portions were used quite effectively on the score of the movie *The Squid and the Whale*.

But it's not just the music that makes *SHR* so great. It's the lyrics, too. They're like the spinach your own mom snuck into a batch of brownies. They're stealthily good for you. Throughout one's entire life in the classroom (and we're not just talking grade school here) *SHR* lyrics provide a mental cheat sheet on a number of important learned topics. So the sooner you introduce this stuff to your child, the better.

Examples: find yourself staring down the business end of a high school pop-quiz on the American constitution? No problem. Just start singing those long ago ingrained lyrics to "The Preamble" which, as it turns out, just so happen to be largely "constituted" of the language found in the preamble to the greatest American document ever produced.

Asked to define for your junior high class the function of an adjective in a sentence? Piece of cake. Just summon the power and glory (and chorus) of that old *SHR* standby "Unpack Your Adjectives."

Fourth grade science teacher thinks he can stump you when he asks you to name all of the planets? No sweat. "Interplanet Janet" ingrained the answers years ago. While *Schoolhouse Rock* no longer airs on television, "Best of" CDs are still around, a thirtieth anniversary DVD is widely available, regional theater productions inspired by the series can still occasionally be found, and, of course, for older kids there's always YouTube.

Most of all, *Schoolhouse Rock* is a great way for mom, dad, and junior to settle the near-impossible-to-solve "let's listen to something we all like" issue on the next family road trip (or grocery store excursion).

Because at the end of the day, when a young family goes about the business of choosing an acceptable highway soundtrack, it does indeed take the consensus of three . . . and that's a magic number!

Ten Songs To Know That We Couldn't Fit in Anywhere Else

(but that we have little to include because even just mentioning them in this headline gets them stuck in our heads again. Thanks a lot.)

"Take Me Out to the Ballgame"

"She'll Be Coming Around the Mountain"

"My Bonny Lies Over the Ocean"

"Old McDonald Had a Farm"

McDonald's jingle parodies, which usually include some variation on hamburgers up one's nose and French fries between one's eyes.

"The Alphabet Song"

"Bingo"

"Alouette"

"The Bear Went Over the Mountain"

"Rock-a-Bye Baby"

Intermezzo: The Ever-Changing, Always-Constant World of Charlie Brown

What could be simpler? A gang of little kids—primarily the brother/sister teams of Charlie Brown/Sally and Linus/Lucy, plus a hyperimaginative dog—go to school, play sports, celebrate the holidays, etc.

Well, it's really much more than that. *Peanuts*—as created by Charles Schulz—took the funny papers, the book world, the land of TV and, to a lesser extent, music and theater, by storm.

We won't bother wasting your time with a who's-who rundown. The *Peanuts* lineup is as well known as Dorothy's *Wizard of Oz* pals. Instead, we'll fill you in on some of the ups and downs in the evolution of the franchise—the better to expose your kid to Snoopy the dog before he's listening to Snoop Dog.

1950: *Peanuts* makes its newspaper debut. Nobody seems too concerned that its main character, Charlie Brown has a big, big head. Seriously. That's one large dome he's got there. The first strip features two kids talking about "good ol' Charlie Brown." After he passes, one says, "How I hate him." So we're starting out with the not-particularly-well-liked main character. But a lot else is different. For one, the kids actually act like kids—something that will change later. (Artist Art Spiegelman has commented, wisely, that all of the characters in Peanuts are adults—except for Snoopy.)

1952: The first *Peanuts* Sunday comic strip appears. Added to the mix: the brother/sister team of Lucy and Linus. She's brutal. He's attached to his blanket. Actually, the blanket doesn't enter the scene for another three years. Interesting how these iconic elements can take time. Charlie Chaplin didn't start with his moustache, hat, and cane, either.

1953: Lucy falls in love with piano-playing Schroeder. You've got to give credit to Schroeder, who resists the advances of the strong-willed Lucy for the next half-century.

1955: Pigpen appears. Every school has a smelly kid. *Peanuts* is the only comic strip to suggest that it was okay for him to be your friend. Kodak licenses the *Peanuts* characters for use in a camera handbook. Let the seemingly endless parade of sponsorships begin. Linus's blanket is introduced.

1956: Snoopy walks erect.

1959: Charlie Brown's sister Sally makes her first appearances—as an infant. Unlike Charlie Brown, she actually ages. At least for a while, then she levels off like the rest. Nobody seems to mind. Comic strip fans are like that.

1959: Lucy begins her discount psychiatric practice.

1960: Hallmark introduces *Peanuts* greeting cards.

1962: The Peanuts book *Happiness is a Warm Puppy* lands on the *New York Times* Bestseller list.

1965: *A Charlie Brown Christmas,* one of the greatest half-hours in the history of television, debuts. Both deeply spiritual and deeply funny, it immortalized the music of Vince Guaraldi.

1966: *It's the Great Pumpkin, Charlie Brown,* one of the other greatest half hours in the history of television, premiers. Charlie Schulz was obviously reading his Samuel Beckett. Also in 1966, "Snoopy vs. the Red Baron" becomes a music hit for The Royal Guardsmen, charting at number two. Schulz and company are, at first, none too pleased, but eventually an agreement is reached. The band later recorded "Snoopy's Christmas," "The Return of the Red Baron," and other attempts to score again—until, the story goes, Schulz told them "enough already." Most recently, the Royal Guardsmen recorded "Snoopy vs. Osama." Nobody seemed to care.

1967: *You're a Good Man, Charlie Brown* opens off-Broadway. The musical stars Gary Burghoff— later to be *M*A*S*H*'s* Radar O'Reilly—as Charlie Brown and Bob Balaban—network head Russell Dalrymple from *Seinfeld— as* Linus. Still one of the most produced shows in regional theaters, *YAGM,CB* effectively captures the philosophical spirit of the early cartoons. But seeing the kids played by adults can be a little jarring. What if, for instance, you find yourself attracted to the woman playing Lucy? Isn't that a little creepy?

Circa 1968: While an exact date is impossible to pin down, this is about the time when an unauthorized image of a pregnant Lucy shouting "Damn you, Charlie Brown!" begins to circulate. The cartoon covers a remarkable amount of ground in a pre-Internet, pre-fax-machine world.

1969: *A Boy Named Charlie Brown,* the first *Peanuts* feature film, is released. Frankly, it's not so good—at least compared to the first batch of television specials. In it, the gang competes in a spelling bee, Charlie Brown goes to the nationals and muffs it when he can't spell "beagle." The title song was written by pop poet Rod McKuen. As far as we know, it wasn't nominated for anything.

1970: The bird Woodstock, who has appeared before, is given a name. This, keep in mind, is just a year after the famed concert.

1971: Snoopy joins the touring "Holiday on Ice" show, paving the way for skating costume characters evermore. *National Lampoon* publishes a "Death is" parody of "Happiness is." Lawyers are soon on the case. Meanwhile, Marcie calls Peppermint Patty "sir." We're not going to even speculate on the impact this has on the gay rights movement.

1972: In *Snoopy Come Home*, we find out that the dog had a previous owner. The who-does-he-belong-with plot predates *Kramer vs. Kramer* by seven years.

1973: *A Charlie Brown Thanksgiving* premiers—the last decent Peanuts TV special. After this, it's stuff like *It's Flashbeagle, Charlie Brown, It's the Girl in the Red Truck, Charlie Brown,* and *Lucy Must Be Traded, Charlie Brown* (all actual titles).

1974: Rerun appears. You never heard of Rerun? Rerun is Linus and Lucy's little brother. Think of him as the Cousin Oliver of *Peanuts*.

1975: *Snoopy!!!: The Musical,* premieres in San Francisco, trying to capture the success of *You're a Good Man, Charlie Brown*. It doesn't. But it was turned into a 1988 animated TV special.

1975: Spike, Snoopy's brother, makes his first appearance. Nobody really seems to care except Snoopy and Charles Schulz.

1976: Everybody stops caring about everything *Peanuts*-related. Or so it seems.

1977: *Race for Your Life Charlie Brown*, the mercifully last Peanuts feature film, is released.

1980: Charles Schulz wins the Charles M. Schulz Award from United Features Syndicate for his contribution to the field of cartooning. Are we the only ones who think that's a little, oh, odd?

1983: Camp Snoopy opens at Knott's Berry Farm amusement park.

1986: The Peanuts gang starts shilling for MetLife insurance. It seems like the end times are at hand.

1989: Olaf debuts. We have no idea who Olaf is and, as an act of protest, we're not going to bother checking.

1999: *You're a Good Man, Charlie Brown* is revived in New York. New songs are written so that Sally can be part of the show.

Anthony Rapp, formerly of *Rent*, plays Charlie Brown. Meanwhile, Charles Schulz retires. Around the same time, MetLife cuts back on its use of the *Peanuts* gang. "I felt it was too much Snoopy," Robert H. Benmosche, chairman, president and chief executive at MetLife in New York told the *New York Times*. "When you talk about MetLife, you say, 'That's Snoopy's company,' and that's important. But we also want the ads to begin to remind people why to do business with MetLife." Whatever.

2000: Charles Schulz dies. The final daily *Peanuts* strip appears. Suddenly, we care again.

Part IV

MOVIES

One of the first assumptions that a new parent makes is that, when it comes to media, Disney equals harmless. When it comes to anything created by Walt, you're not only getting entertainment, your getting something that's suitable for the whole family at any age.

Sorry to shatter that illusion. The Disney universe is a multifaceted one. And since you'll be spending a lot of time in it, we thought we'd give you some insight on the MPAA ratings system, then get rolling by digging deep into the Disney universe with a look at the entire Disney animated canon.

We'll also look at the rest of the kid-movie world, including nonanimated Disney, non-Disney animation, animation/live action hybrids, computer-animated flicks, and more.

There's a lot of great stuff out there, a lot of junk, and a lot in between. Instead of your conscience, let us be your guide. (Oh, okay, your conscience can be part of this, too.)

What's in a Rating?

You are, no doubt, familiar with the motion picture ratings systems:

G for "General Audiences."

PG for "Parental Guidance Suggested."

PG-13 for "Parents Strongly Cautioned. Some Material May be Inappropriate for Children under 13."

R for "Restricted. Under 17 Requires Accompanying Parent or Guardian."

And, well, you probably haven't heard too much lately about NC-17 because, rather than get slapped with it, most filmmakers would rather cut their film down to an R. Many newspapers won't carry an ad for an NC-17 film. Most video stores won't carry it. And none of the NC-17 business matters to you right now because you're a parent and this is a section focusing on kid films.

What may be confusing as you select films that might or might not be okay for your kid to watch: ratings didn't exist prior to 1968. Since there was a self-regulation system in place back then, the DVD cases of, say, *20,000 Leagues Under the Sea* and *Frankenstein Meets the Wolfman* don't really clue you in on which was okay for your kid and which wasn't.

At first, the ratings consisted of G, M, R and X, which didn't work out too well because parents assumed that M (for Mature) was worse than R (for Restricted). M became first GP (General Audiences: Parental guidance suggested) and then, a year later, flipped to PG. You might still see a stray GP rating here and there as you look into rentable films. More than likely, though, you'll see that these have been reclassified to either PG (as was the caper film *The Doberman Gang*) or to R (see the decidedly not-tyke-friendly *A Man Called Horse*).

In 1984, thanks in large part to Steven Spielberg grossing people out with *Indiana Jones and the Temple of Doom*, the PG rating was split into two: PG and PG-13. The latter encouraged parents to seriously consider not taking their ten-year-olds to *Red Dawn, Johnny Dangerously,* and *The Woman in Red.*

At the same time, though, PG-13 encouraged makers of R-rated films to trim a little to make a film available to the widest possible audience.

In 1990, things changed a little more. X became NC-17. And, more relevant here, explanatory words were added to R-rated films to explain why the rating was given. Later, these descriptors were also added to PG-13 and NC-17 films.

Who decides on a film's rating? A Los Angeles–based rating board known as the Motion Picture Association of America (MPAA). According to the late Jack Valenti, who spearheaded the rating system, the board and its members represent "parenthood experience . . . and intelligent maturity and . . . the capacity to put themselves in the role of most American parents so they can view a film and apply a rating that most parents would find suitable and helpful in aiding their decisions about their children's moviegoing."

There is no obligation, by the way, for a film to be submitted to the ratings board. You'll find plenty of unrated films on Netflix, most of which bypassed theaters completely and went straight to video.

And be warned: just because you are taking your kid to a PG movie doesn't mean there won't be trailers for R rated films. The MPAA doles out "all audiences" or "restricted audiences" approval for trailers based on whether or not any scenes shown in the trailer itself caused the feature to earn its non-G rating.

The Disney Animated-Feature Canon Part 1: The Walt Years

At the risk of being exhaustive (and exhausting), we now present a rundown of every official Disney feature animated film that's been released in theaters. We've excluded stuff like *Jungle Book II*, which isn't officially a part of the Disney canon. (Plus, we really didn't want to sit through *Jungle Book II* again.)

SNOW WHITE AND THE SEVEN DWARVES

The basics: Girl meets prince. Girl booted out of castle by the quintessential evil stepmother. Girl meets dwarves. Stepmother tries to kill girl with poison apple. Prince (and dwarves) save girl.

Nutshell Messages: Apples are bad. Kisses can save you. Little old men can be okay. Someday your prince will come.

Fun Fact: Credited with being the first full-length animated film, it was actually long predated by the 1917 Argentinean film "The Apostle." Don't search Netflix for it, though—no known copies exist.

Why to Watch: 1. Historical value (while it isn't the first feature-length animated film, it is the first *American* feature-length animated film, which is all that really matters). 2. A couple of good tunes (the ones not sung exclusively by

SW, including "Heigh-Ho" and "Whistle While You Work."). 3. So that you can win a bar bet with other drinking parents by naming all of the dwarfs.

Why to Avoid: You'll want to grab for the remote when SW sings, and cover your kid's eyes when the witch does her thing. Remember: there's a reason why the ride at Disney World is called "Snow White's Scary Adventure" and has warnings attached to it. To wit: when the film premiered in England, it was deemed too scary for children, and those under 16 had to be accompanied by an adult.

Advice: Proceed with caution.

PINOCCHIO

The Basics: Benevolent Italian toymaker wishes upon a star that his "little wooden head" puppet will transform into a real boy. A blue fairy meets him halfway and brings the puppet to life. A full transformation lies with Pinocchio's ability to prove himself an honest and trustworthy lad. Standing in his way? A variety of shady characters and a nose that just keeps on a-growin'.

Nutshell Messages: Always let your conscience be your guide. Lying is bad. An "actor's life" is dangerous. Ditto a whale's belly. Real boys are "brave, truthful, and unselfish." Blue Fairies are kinda hot.

Fun Fact: Mel Blanc, who famously voiced Loony Tunes characters Bugs Bunny, Daffy Duck, Porky Pig, and others was hired to voice Gideon the Cat. The dialogue he recorded was eventually scrapped when it was decided the character would be mute.

Why to Watch: Considered by many film historians to be the high water mark in animation from a technical point of view, the film's use of color and shadow is a sight to behold. Plus, "When You Wish Upon a Star" is one catchy little ditty.

Movies

Why to Avoid: The Pleasure Island sequence, in which Pinocchio and other youngsters indulge in pool hall tomfoolery, destruction of property, drinking, smoking, and other assorted acts of debauchery, is extremely dark and more than a tad unsettling. When the boys' excesses cause them to be transformed into donkeys, the whole thing becomes downright capital-C Creepy.

Advice: It's a gorgeous film. But a couple scenes are perhaps best left for those who appreciate cinematic beauty and don't have to, say, tuck anyone in at night. Your remote has a fast-forward button. There are a couple times you'll be inclined to use it.

FANTASIA

The Basics: Disney creates animated music videos from classical music pieces.

Nutshell Message: Music that's good for you might impress your parents, but it makes for probably the least interesting Disney flick for kids.

Fun Fact: Dopey, from *Snow White and the Seven Dwarves,* was originally considered for the lead in the "Sorcerer's Apprentice" segment.

Why to Watch: You've bought into the whole "Baby Mozart" business and you want to continue exposing your kid to classical music. The "Dance of the Hours" hippos are fun, and "The Sorcerer's Apprentice" still holds up.

Why to Avoid: It loses its power and is easily tuned out on a small screen.

Advice: The "Night on Bald Mountain" demon is pretty scary. But you'll all be asleep by then.

DUMBO

The Basics: A baby elephant is delivered to his mother at the circus. Cute kid. Massive ears. Other elephants nickname him Dumbo. Mother goes nuts. Kid gets ostracized. Befriends a smart mouse. Learns how to fly. Mother and son together again.

Nutshell Messages: One man (or beast's) handicap is another man (or beast's) wings. Your mommy loves you and always will. Where do babies come from? The stork, silly.

Fun Fact: Timothy Mouse's comment: "Lots of people with big ears are famous!" is said to be an inside joke about Walt Disney himself, who did, in fact, have oversized ears.

Why to Watch: Clocking in at a quick and easy sixty-four minutes (making it the shortest single-segmented Disney animated feature) with a straightforward narrative and likeable main character, *Dumbo* is as good a film as any to introduce your child to the wonderful world of Disney.

Why to Avoid: You might have some explaining to do when Dumbo and Timothy drink the "funny water" that causes them to hiccup, pass out in a tree, and imagine the trippy "Pink Elephants on Parade" sequence that, by the way, kind of overstays its welcome.

Advice: Note to moms especially: Have some tissues on hand for the "Baby Mine" sequence.

BAMBI

The Basics: The future Great Prince of the Forest—a baby white-tailed deer—is born and a bunch of furry animals come to check him out. The young lad spends a whole lotta quality time with mom learning about the ways of the woods and such. Mom meets her maker. Bambi grows up, falls in love, and discovers once again that man is the most vicious of all beasts. But family life has a way of making things better. For now, anyway.

Nutshell Messages: If you can't say something nice, don't say nothin' at all. Man in the forest equals big trouble. Eating greens is a special treat—it makes long ears and great big feet (but it sure is awful stuff to eat). Winter seems long but it won't last forever. Springtime is for lovers. Mothers are caring. Fathers are emotionally unavailable. Ice is slippery.

Fun Fact: The offscreen villain "man" was ranked the number 20 movie villain of all time on the American Film Institute's list of heroes and villains.

Why to Watch: It's a great-looking film populated with accessible childlike characters, including Thumper the rabbit and a skunk named Flower.

Why to Avoid: Because when Bambi's mom is shot and killed by "man," even adults will find the whole thing more than a little unsettling.

Advice: Wait a few years. When your child starts to inquire about death and the afterlife, maybe it's finally the right time to bring him to uncontrollable tears with this classic piece of "entertainment," which *Time* magazine appropriately named one of the top twenty-five horror films of all-time.

SALUDOS AMIGOS

The Basics: Walt Disney tries to make friends in South America.

Nutshell Message: Boy, those South-of-the-Border folks are sure colorful.

Fun Fact: Its foreign-language release came before its English one.

Why to Watch: You've never been to South America.

Why to Avoid: Because it's little more than four mediocre shorts strung together with documentary footage and marks the beginning of Disney's attempt, despite the failure of *Bambi*, to keep *something* in theaters.

Advice: salte-o

THE THREE CABALLEROS

Kind of like *Saludos Amigos*, but with Donald Duck along for the trip.

MAKE MINE MUSIC

The Basics: In this, Disney's eighth animated feature, fittingly there are eight segments set to music from Benny Goodman, Dinah Shore, Nelson Eddy, and others.

Nutshell Messages: Wolves are dangerous. Hats? Amorous. Whales can sing. Arrogant heroes strike out. Music is special.

Fun Fact: Sterling Holloway, who famously gave voice to Winnie the Pooh, here narrates the Casey at the Bat segment.

Why to Watch: The Peter and The Wolf and Casey at the Bat segments hold up well enough. And both have solid lessons. The former teaches youngsters about musical motifs and how instruments have their own "voices." The latter, based on the famous poem, shows that arrogance can lead to one's downfall.

Why to Avoid: Made during World War II, when much of Disney's animation department was either drafted or working on propaganda films, this package film comprised of unrelated musical segments looks and feels like the product of a depleted staff.

Advice: Skip it. While there's really nothing here to worry about in terms of age appropriateness, there's nothing particularly special or memorable about any of it.

FUN AND FANCY FREE

The Basics: Another Disney compilation, including *Bongo*–about a circus bear in the wild–and *Mickey and the Beanstalk*, another attempt to revive the popularity of the mouse.

Nutshell Message: If you are looking for messages here, you've come to the wrong place.

Fun Fact: The first Mickey Mouse film in which he wasn't voiced by Walt Disney.

Why to Watch: There was nothing else at your local lending library (we're confident you aren't actually

Movies

paying to rent this one).

Why to Avoid: You've got better things to do.

Verdict: Not necessary.

MELODY TIME

The Basics: This movie features seven sequences set to popular, folk, and classical music. Some are based on American legends like Johnny Appleseed and Pecos Bill, while others are more . . . oh, how to describe? Let's call them "fancifully abstract." Two of the pieces were repurposed and augmented with a John Henry short to make up the DVD *Walt Disney's American Legends*.

Nutshell Messages: Tugboats, like little engines before them, also "can." Cowboys rock. Sambas roll. Some tall tales and legends never get old. When you've got great music, you don't need as many pesky words.

Fun Fact: Donald Duck's middle name is Fauntleroy.

Why to Watch: Donald Duck and Roy Rogers in the same movie? Sweet! But look, the honest truth is this film is a bit of an odd hodge-podge with some parts (i.e. "Little Toot" featuring the Andrews Sisters in their usual solid voice) working better than others (i.e. a sequence based on the poem "Trees." What the . . . ?) none of which gel into a cohesive whole. Still, there are style points to be had for attempting to break out of your household's seen-it-a-hundred-times-and-growing rotation. Plus, did we mention Donald Duck and Roy Rogers in the same movie?

Why to Avoid: Because the in-your-face Christianity message of the Johnny Appleseed segment feels a bit out of place. Because when it comes to introducing unknown and non-linear movies to your child, there are only so many battles you can fight. Because *Fantasia* does the same kind of thing a whole lot better.

Advice: Best left for the die-hardiest Disney fan.

THE ADVENTURES OF ICHABOD AND MR. TOAD

The Basics: Disney still treading water with a for-no-particular-reason pairing of *The Wind and the Willows* and *The Legend of Sleepy Hollow* adaptations.

Nutshell Message: Buying cars can lead to major debt. Just because a guy is headless doesn't mean he can't have a good throwing arm.

Fun Fact: After this compilation flick, Disney goes back to making single-subject animated films. Thank goodness.

Why to Watch: Er, is your kid is a fan of Bing Crosby (who narrates the Sleepy Hollow story)?

Why to Avoid: Two words: *Headless* and *Horseman*.

Advice: Skip.

CINDERELLA

The Basics: When a beautiful young maiden's father dies, her stepmother and two stepsisters reveal their true, evil colors. Poor Cinderella is now forced to do their bidding. A prince needs a wife. A ball is planned. A Fairy Godmother hooks Cindy up with some fancy garb. The clock strikes midnight. Cindy loses her slipper. She later gets it back, plus the prince to boot.

Nutshell Messages: A dream is a wish your heart makes. Stepmothers suck. Mice are friendly. Cats are evil. Even miracles take a little time. If the shoe fits . . .

Fun Fact: Cinderella is commonly pictured wearing a blue ball gown in Disney merchandise. The ball gown she wears in the film is in fact silver and white.

Why to Watch: A kind-hearted heroine. Snappy tunes. Good messages about keeping your chin up through tough times, following your dreams, and the life-changing power finding the perfect dress can bring.

Why to Avoid: Evil stepmother

stereotype might confuse your impressionable tike. As might the prefeminist "man-can-save-you" assumptions. The mice and the cat log more screen time than they probably deserve. Weird foot fetish motif.

Advice: It's a good film with a happy ending (the appropriate-for-children kind).

ALICE IN WONDERLAND

The Basics: A young girl chases a white rabbit and finds the ever curiouser and curiouser world of Wonderland. A bunch of trippy adventures ensue, including: eating and drinking things that make her grow very tall and very small; tea with a Mad Hatter; painting roses red; an unusual game of croquet. But no worries. It's all a dream.

Nutshell Messages: Don't be late for a very important date. Most days are very merry unbirthdays.

"Be patient" is very good advice. All ways are the Queen's ways. Remember what the dormouse said: Feed Your Head. Feed Your Head. Or just say no. Either way.

Fun Fact: The movie includes sixteen songs, more than any other Disney animated film.

Why to Watch: Eschewing a tightly constructed narrative, the terrific visuals and music are the chief sources of entertainment.

Why to Avoid: Eschewing a tightly constructed narrative, the terrific visuals and music are the chief sources of entertainment.

Advice: Perhaps best left for older kids with active imaginations—and liberal arts college students with too much time on their hands.

PETER PAN

The Basics: An adventurous boy, who refuses to grow up, stealthily visits the Darling family's London home. Loses his shadow. Gets it back. Finds the Darling children—

Wendy, Michael and John—are up for some adventure. So it's off to Neverland. Encounters with Pirates, Indians, Mermaids and "Lost Boys" ensue.

Nutshell Messages: Fairies are jealous. Crocodiles? Relentless. Youth is ephemeral (unless, of course, you consistently travel past the second star to the right and straight on 'til morning. In which case, youth is everlasting.) Life is cyclical, i.e. "All this has happened before and it will all happen again."

Fun Fact: Hans Conreid voices both Captain Hook and Mr. Darling—one of the few traditions from J. M. Barrie's original stage play that Disney honors in the film.

Why to Watch: Neverland is filled with wonder, adventure, and enough pixie dust to keep the party rolling 'til dawn. Plus, it's hard to resist bumbling pirates and the Pan's swashbuckling brand of youthful insouciance.

Why to Avoid: The stereotype-laden depiction of Native Americans in the "What Makes the Red Man Red" sequence makes enlightened modern audiences want to say, well, "ugg." Moreover, despite the fact that Tinkerbell is one of Disney's most iconic characters, this sprightly little pixie—with her homicidal tendencies, body issues, and visible panties—subtly adds the "P" to a so-called "G"-rated character.

Advice: You should fly, you should fly, you should fly, you should fly, you should fly! (or drive—whatever's easiest) to your local video store to rent this, one of Disney's most beloved classics—although typical of an era when Disney seemed to have given up on creating art and instead shifted to entertainment.

LADY AND THE TRAMP

The Basics: A well-to-do couple adopt a pretty cocker spaniel puppy and shower her with love and attention. Until, that is, a baby enters the picture. Lady gets the cold shoulder on the home front and turns to the footloose and fancy-free Tramp for help, adventure, spaghetti for two, and eventually love.

Nutshell Messages: Money can't buy the wag of a dog's tail. Puppies are a young couple's baby tryout. Pasta is an aphrodisiac. Siamese cats are mischievous. Rats? Evil. Family life is more fulfilling than bachelorhood. They're called man's best friend for a reason.

Fun Fact: Singer/songwriter Peggy Lee successfully sued Disney over video rights and was awarded $2.3 million thirty-six years after the film's initial release.

Why to Watch: Likeable characters from the titular leads to the "Trusty" sidekicks to the scene-stealing Siamese cats. Enough action to temper the romance. The "Bella Notte" sequence outside of Tony's restaurant is as iconic and romantic a scene as has ever been put on film.

Why to Avoid: Let's see. Umm, well, if you're not a "dog person," this probably isn't the best choice for you. And if your child really, really, really hates spaghetti, then that might put a damper on his or her enjoyment of the movie's signature moment.

Advice: About as doggone good as almost anything in the Disney canon.

SLEEPING BEAUTY

The Basics: A king and queen bring a baby daughter into the kingdom and quickly betroth her to a young prince. The party gets all buzz-killed when the "mistress of all evil" curses her to die by her sixteenth birthday. A fairy changes the death curse thing into a sleep curse thing, reversible only by true love's kiss. Take one guess how the rest plays out.

Nutshell Messages: If you dream it, you can do it. Fairies rule! A good forty winks or so can do wonders for one's life. True love conquers all.

Fun Fact: Animators had Audrey Hepburn in mind when they created Princess Aurora's long and thin body shape.

Why to Watch: With a more stylized look than its fairy tale-based predecessors and a beautiful score partially adopted from Tchaikovsky's *Sleeping Beauty Ballet*, the film has all the hall-marks of a classic Disney Princess movie: Dreaming big dreams, singing with birds, flirting with the future Mr. Right, the defeating of evil, and dancing the big happily-ever-after waltz.

Why to Avoid: When the wicked Maleficent delivers her death curse with a heavy emphasis on the words "AND DIE!" she makes Hannibal Lecture and other famous movie villains seem like, well, Disney characters. So there's that. Also, if you're trying to instill some progressive thinking in your little one about modern gender roles, you could most certainly find better examples than what's being presented here.

Advice: Probably a good idea to watch with your young 'un first to see if she (and you) can handle the darker scenes. Plus, this way you can explain upfront that if this movie were made today, it's very likely the prince is the one who would need saving.

101 DALMATIANS

The Basics: Pair of spotted dogs bring human couple together. The Dalmatian couple has a boatload of pups and then, after the kids are kidnapped, find tenfold more. Eventually, they all escape the clutches of Cruella deVille.

Nutshell Message: Parents will do anything for their kids.

Fun Fact: The first Disney animated film to be remade as a live-action film. And one of the rare Disney films with an intact traditional (albeit animal) family at its core through to the end of the movie.

Why to Watch: For proof that a Disney film didn't have to be a musical to be a classic.

Why to Avoid: Cruella is pretty Creepella, to boot.

Advice: Definitely see it before you inflict the live-action version on your kids.

THE SWORD IN THE STONE

The Basics: When the King of England dies, no one is quite sure who should take over the throne. Until, that is, a sword appears in a stone stating that the one who removes it is the one who gets the gig. Cut to: a wizard meets a young boy. Likes the lad. Decides to home-school him. Changes the boy into various creatures in the name of education. Boy pulls the sword from the stone. Long live the king.

Nutshell Messages: "For every high there is a low. For every to there is a fro." Brains trump brawn. Female squirrels are horny. Dishes pile up. Magic won't solve all your problems. Looks can be deceiving.

Fun Fact: Richard and Robert Reitherman were hired to voice Arthur after original Arthur Rickie Sorensen's voice changed. If you listen carefully, you can hear the "changed voice" go back to an "unchanged voice." The Reitherman boys are brothers to Bruce Reitherman, the voice of Mowgli and Christopher Robin in subsequent Disney films.

Why to Watch: Nice way to introduce your youngster to the legend of King Arthur. Decent animation. Solid messages about the value of a good mentor and buckling down on the books.

Why to Avoid: The sword goes in up front, the sword comes out in the end. Everything in between is just sort of filler. The only real villain is Merlin's nemesis, Madam Mim, who appears late and is disposed of quickly. Plus, no romance? Limited action?

Songs? Who's this movie for, anyway?

Advice: Worth adding to your Netflix queue. But there are a couple dozen Disney films to put before it.

THE JUNGLE BOOK

The Basics: A young baby is found in a basket deep in the jungles of India. He's raised by wolves and learns to love his surroundings. When he grows older it's decided he should live in the man village where he will be safe from the villainous tiger, Shere Khan. On the way he meets many colorful characters, learns the bear necessities, and watches a bunch of simians get down.

Nutshell Messages: Bears know the necessities. Elephants are militant. Snakes aren't trustworthy. Orangutans can party. Panthers are friends. Tigers are enemies. Man cubs are suckers for water-fetchers with doe eyes. When you pick a paw-paw or a prickly pear and you prick a raw paw next time beware.

Fun Fact: Or, in this case, not-so-fun fact. This was the last feature film produced by Walt Disney, who died during its production. On a happier—if, later, abused—note, it's also the first Disney film where most of its voice talent (including Phil Harris and Louie Prima) was already well known outside of the world of animation.

Why to Watch: It's one of Disney's most popular films, and it's easy to see why. Great characters, songs, and animation. Plus, it's the first Disney film in which the human protagonist is not Caucasian—a harbinger of more colorful Disney heroes to come.

Why to Avoid: Shere Khan is an intense tiger. Baloo briefly seems dead.

Advice. Don't just rent it, buy it. You'll be watching it for years to come.

Movies

The Disney Princesses Quiz

And so we take a break from the Disney film-by-film analysis for a brief quiz to see how much you know about those gown-wearing gals from the WD kingdom.

1. There are eight official Disney Princesses. Name Them. (1 point each)

2. Which princess was not a princess by birth?
a) Snow White
b) Belle
c) Jasmine
d) Aurora

3. Which Disney Princess never technically becomes a "real" princess by bloodline or marriage?
a) Mulan
b) Ariel
c) Pocahontas
d) Belle

4. Which Princess has both her parents alive?
a) Cinderella
b) Ariel
c) Snow White
d) Mulan

5. True or False:
One of the Disney Princesses was voiced by a man.

6. Only one Disney Princess wears a crown. Which one?
a) Belle
b) Cinderella
c) Ariel
d) Aurora

7. Match the Disney Princess with her animal sidekick (1 point for each correct answer)
Tiger _____
Horse _____
Hummingbird _____
Mice _____
Fish _____

8. What is Belle's father's name?
a) Mitchell
b) Michael
c) Maurice
d) Maury

9. Who is the only Disney Princess that is not the main character of her movie? _____.

10. What are the names of the fairies who raise Princess Aurora?
a) Flora, Fauna, and Merryweather
b) Drizella, Anastasia, and Tremaine
c) Flounder, Sebastian, and Scuttle
d) Dopey, Grumpy, and Doc

11. Which two Disney Princesses have a grandmother?
a) Cinderella and Aurora
b) Pochantas and Mulan
c) Ariel and Belle
d) Snow White and Jasmine

12. Which princess does not have brown eyes?
a) Pocahontas
b) Belle
c) Ariel
d) Jasmine

Movies

13 Which Princess's name means "little mischief?"

a) Belle

b) Mulan

c) Aurora

d) Pocahantas

14. True or False: The Castle at Disneyland is called Cinderella's Castle.

15. Which Disney princess has the most number of siblings?

a) Cinderella

b) Jasmine

c) Ariel

d) Mulan

16. Which Disney Princess has the longest hair?

a) Jasmine

b) Aurora

c) Pocahontas

d) Belle

17. Which Disney Princesses are seen barefoot at some point in their movie?

a) Cinderella and Pocahontas

b) Cinderella and Ariel

c) None of them

d) All of them

18. True or False: No Disney Princess wears pants.

19. Which Disney Princess doesn't cry during her movie?

a) Snow White

b) Ariel

c) Mulan

d) Pocahontas

20. Match the princess with her corresponding lyrics (1 point for each correct answer)

"I want adventure in the great wide somewhere/I want it more than I can tell"

"Up where they walk/Up where they run/Up where they stay all day in the sun"

"No matter how your heart is grieving/if you keep on believing/the dream that you wish will come true"

"Some day when spring is here/We'll find our love anew/And the birds will sing/And wedding bells will ring "

"And I know it's true that visions are seldom all they seem/But if I know you, I know what you do/You love me at once, the way you did once upon a dream"

21. Which Disney princess do we see as a baby?
a) Cinderella
b) Snow White
c) Aurora
d) Jasmine

22. Which Disney Princess does not dance with a prince?
a) Ariel
b) Cinderella
c) Mulan
d) Jasmine

23. True or False: Maleficent is the name of Cinderella's Fairy God Mother.

24. Aurora's dress changes from blue to pink several times in her movie. What color is it when the movie ends?

25. Which princess is not married at the end of her movie?
a) Belle
b) Jasmine
c) Cinderella
d) Ariel

The Disney Animated Feature Canon Part 2: The Post-Walt Years

We're back, this time with the low-down on the Disney animated features released after Disney's death.

THE ARISTOCATS

The Basics: Cat and her three kittens on the lam in Paris.

Nutshell Message: Everybody wants to be a cat. Don't be a snob.

Fun Fact: The first feature animated film completed without Walt Disney himself. But we already told you that.

Why to Watch: Although it can feel like a retread of *Lady and the Tramp, The Aristocats* features good-enough songs, good-enough drama, and good-enough characters to hold up on its own.

Why to Avoid: The moment in "Everybody Wants to be a Cat" where the Paul Winchell–voiced feline puts the cymbal on his head and does the most condescending impersonation of an Asian since Mickey Rooney in *Breakfast at Tiffany's*. Also, if you aren't paying close attention, you may find yourself with a copy of *The Aristocrats,* perhaps the most foul-language-filled film of all time.

ROBIN HOOD

The Basics: With taxes high and morale low in not-exactly-jolly-old-England (Nottingham, more specifically), a rogue community hero robs the rich to feed the poor, woos the comely Maid Merion, and becomes the maddening bane of the phony King John's existence.

Nutshell Messages: Crime is a matter of perspective. Men are merry. Ineffective monarchs have mommy issues. Most problems can be solved with a bow and arrow. "Ooda-lolly" is an underrated catch phrase.

Fun Fact: The sound of church bells ringing at the end of the film is a recycled sound clip from *Cinderella*.

Why to Watch: Likeable characters. A lot of good old-fashioned swashbuckling. The Baloolike Little John. Big fun. Roger Miller making an art out of good old-fashioned whistling.

Why to Avoid: Of all of Disney's animated feature films, this is one of the most superficial in terms of both visual execution and plot. With the love interests already in love before we meet them and a villain so inept he's almost sympathetic, the story lacks the kind of narrative tension we've come to expect from Uncle Walt & Company.

Advice: Still, it's a pleasant enough diversion, which presents absolutely zilch for parents to worry about in terms of scariness or the inappropriateness factors.

THE MANY ADVENTURES OF WINNIE THE POOH

The basics: A. A. Milne's stuffed bear of very little brain goes searching for honey, survives a blustery day, and gets himself into and out of other adventures with his friends from the 100-Acre Wood.

Nutshell messages: Mmmmm, honey! Nature is enchanting and sometimes a little scary. The wonderful thing about Tiggers? Uh, duh. Tiggers are wonderful things! There's nothing more comforting than knowing your bestest friends will always have your back.

Fun fact: Winnie the Pooh features and merchandise reportedly outearn the revenue of Mickey Mouse, Minnie Mouse, Pluto, and Goofy combined!

Why to Watch: In this classic— actually a compilation of three *Pooh* short subjects: *Winnie the Pooh and the Honey Tree* (1966), *Winnie the Pooh and the Blustery Day* (1968), and *Winnie the Pooh and Tigger, Too* (1974)—you won't find a more endearing cast of characters (or for that matter, the voice talent behind them) anywhere in the Disney Universe.

Why to Avoid: There are times when the narrative moves along about as fast as the bear for which it's named. Children accustomed to a lot of action and excitement in their entertainment might find "the willy, nilly, silly old bear" to be a bit of a bore.

Advice: Oh, bother? No way. Bother yourself and your little one silly with this timeless 'toon treasure.

THE RESCUERS

The Basics: A couple of mice from the Rescue Aid Society—a kind of rodent U.N.—are called upon to, well, rescue a little girl captured by Madame Medusa.

Nutshell Message: No matter the obstacle, a good heart can get through it all.

Fun Fact: Although not held in particularly high regard, this was a needed hit for Disney . . . and would be its last animated hit until *The Little Mermaid* twelve years later.

Why to Watch: Bob Newhart as Bernard.

Why to Avoid: It's one thing when the Dalmatians get kidnapped. It's another when a real (or, at least,

animatedly real) kid gets nabbed.
Advice: A good one to pull out of the collection when you and your kid are tired of the ones you know backwards and forwards.

THE FOX AND THE HOUND

The Basics: Tod is a young red fox. Copper is a young bloodhound. They become fast friends, unaware that society says they shouldn't be. As they grow older, a bloodthirsty hunter and his dog, Chief, do their best to turn the animals against each other.

Nutshell Messages: Prejudice is bad. Careful who you choose as your role model. Don't screw with widows. "Big Mama" equals big fun. Find education or find elimination. "Time has a way of changing things."

Fun Fact: It's the last Disney film to end the proceedings with the words "The End." All subsequent films have closing credits.

Why to Watch: Solid messages about tolerance and friendship. Young F&H provide relatable onscreen surrogates for young viewers.

Why to Avoid: The musical numbers are mediocre at best. Tod's mom meets her maker just after the opening credits, so there may be some explaining to do before your seat's even warm. Which is kind of a drag. Paul Winchell, who famously and memorably voices Tigger, here lends his talents to a bird name Dinky—only he does his whole Tigger shtick including the signature laugh. It's very distracting. Kids liable to be depressed by the ending for days. Maybe weeks.

Advice: We don't usually recommend the made-for-video sequels, but in this case have *Fox and the Hound II* on hand and ready, should your kid be weeping uncontrollably.

Movies

THE BLACK CAULDRON

The Basics: According to legend, a king so evil no prison could hold him is captured in a great black cauldron. The cauldron is hidden, since its powers can resurrect an army of undead warriors. Years later an evil horned king attempts to find the cauldron to literally unleash its mean-spiritedness. Standing in his way is a young "assistant pig farmer"-turned-hero named Taran and his new pals Princess Eilonwy, a minstrel named Fflewddur Flam, a creature named Gurgi and a pig with magical powers.

Nutshell Messages: "War is no game. People get hurt." Pigs are special. Apples are tempting. Swords are helpful. If done right, this whole *Lord-of-the-Rings-*meets-Dungeons-and-Dragons fantasy stuff never gets old.

Fun Fact: Due to the graphic nature of the first cut of the film, several scenes were removed due to fears it would be given a PG-13 rating. Also, the first Disney animated film without at least some kind of musical interludes.

Why to Watch: One of the more forgotten films in the Disney canon, it's actually a surprisingly decent, if not typical, Disney film. If nothing else, give it points for making a pig, of all creatures, the one with the special magical powers. This pig makes that Wilbur from *Charlotte's Web* seem like a run-of-the-mill porker. "Some Pig" indeed.

Why to Avoid: It was made to attract teens and preteens interested in the 1980s burgeoning genres of fantasy novels, games, and films, and it shows. A bit too dark for young ones. And where's the music? Seriously, not even one snappy ditty about dragons or brimstone or something?

Advice: Wait several years. And hopefully then, you'll manage to remember this film even exists.

THE GREAT MOUSE DETECTIVE

The Basics: A Sherlock Holmes/Dr. Watson-ish duo solve a crime in London.

Nutshell Message: Smarts beats brawn.

Fun Fact: Alan Young, who voices Hirum Flaversham, was the human buddy of TV's talking horse, Mr. Ed.

Why to Watch: Hmmm . . . well, maybe you really like Vincent Price.

Why to Avoid: Because adults can never quite grasp the fact that kids just aren't that into Sherlock Holmes. Because this is Disney treading water until it comes up with a decent idea.

Advice: No harm but no real reason to pick it up either.

OLIVER & COMPANY

The Basics: Loosely based on Charles Dickens's *Oliver Twist*, a young kitten finds himself orphaned on the streets of New York City. Befriends a street-smart mutt named Dodger, who shows him the ropes. Takes up with Dodger's gang until a better offer comes along in the form of well-to-do and loving little girl named Penny. Gets kidnapped. Sees Penny get kidnapped. It's up to Dodger, his pals, and their owner Fagin to save the day.

Nutshell Messages: "It's always once upon a time in New York City." Money doesn't buy happiness, friends do. Old debts die hard. Never do business with a man named Sikes.

Fun Fact: Blink and you'll miss 'em, but early in the film Jock, Trusty, and Peg from *Lady and the Tramp* make cameo appearances.

Why to Watch: Once you get used to it, it's kind of an interesting change of pace to watch a Disney movie take place in modern times (product placement and all). Cheech Marin shines as Tito.

Why to Avoid: There's a reason why it's considered a (luke)

Movies

warm-up to the great run of films that would follow it: from the animation to the plot to the music it's decidedly average on all fronts. Why Billy Joel was hired as one of the key leads but only given one song to sing is sort of a mystery. And given how his peers Elton John and Phil Collins fared at scoring later films (Hello, Oscars!), you gotta wonder how things could have gone if the Piano Man had been asked to get busy at his piano. Instead there's a song contribution from . . . Barry Manilow?

Advice: When your kid's a little older, rent the live-action musical *Oliver!* Now there's a film with some great tunes.

THE LITTLE MERMAID

The Basics: Mermaid loves boy. Mermaid loses tail. Mermaid gets boy.

Nutshell Message: Follow your heart. Even when your dad is mad, he loves you.

Fun Fact: In his bestseller *The DaVinci Code*, Dan Brown makes a case that Ariel represented Mary Magdalene—although he gets the name of the painting in Ariel's treasure trove wrong. It's Georges de la Tour's "Magdalene with the Smoking Flame."

Why to Watch: Because it's a great movie with, until this point in time, the best Disney score. There are engaging characters, magical music sequences, big laughs, and an equally big heart.

Why to Avoid: No reason in the world. Okay, so the shark attack early in the film is a little scary and the climactic Sea Witch battle is out of proportion with the rest of the film.

Advice: A must-have in your permanent collection.

THE RESCUERS DOWN UNDER

The Basics: That same pair of mice we mentioned a little while back—the ones from the Rescue Aid Society—are called upon to rescue a little boy in the Australian outback.

Nutshell Message: You don't have to be big and powerful to be a hero.

Fun Fact: Until Disney started pillaging its vaults for follow-ups (*Jungle Book II* et al.), this was its first feature animated sequel. So why pick one of its lesser known properties? Beats us. What we do know, though, is that this was the first Disney animated film colored entirely by computer (no more hand-painted cels), and you can see lots of visual experimentation happening on screen.

Why to Watch: A spectacular opening tracking shot. Some great supporting animal characters include a kangaroo rat, a lizard, and of course, a koala, all of whom could have broken out and had some pop culture afterlife if they were featured in a Disney musical.

Why to Avoid: An intensely scary, gun-toting George C. Scott as the villain.

Advice: Really an achievement, but still curiously skipable—like a lot of talent was spent on something that nobody particularly needed or wanted.

BEAUTY AND THE BEAST

The Basics: Bookish girl teaches transformed prince how to love. Providing the assist is a curious group of servants-turned-household items.

Nutshell Message: Don't judge a person by his furry cover. Think before you act. When you're told not to go into the West Wing, well, you still might want to go there anyway.

Fun Fact: Nominated for a Best Picture Oscar and the first animated film to rake in $100 million at the box office.

Why to Watch: Because this Academy Award Best Picture–nominated film isn't just one of the greatest animated musicals of

all time, it's one of the greatest movie musicals of all time. Heck, we'll say it: it's one of the greatest movies of all time.
Why to Avoid: Hmmm. Okay. Well . . . there are some scary wolves.
Advice: Essential.

ALADDIN

The Basics: Young commoner—assisted by a genie—wins a princess and a kingdom.
Nutshell Message: Be yourself. (Haven't we covered this already?)
Fun Fact: The opening song was changed after Arab-American groups reacted badly to such lines as " . . . where they cut off your ear if they don't like your face . . ." and "it's barbaric, but hey, it's home." Both are on the original theatrical release and on the original soundtrack album.
Why to Watch: Up to this point, it's one of the few Disney films with a human boy hero. Okay, that's not really a reason to watch,

but it's sort of interesting. The main reason to watch is because this is a funny, exciting adventure.
Why to Avoid: As with *The Little Mermaid*, the ending is a bit too big. Plus, it does seem a little odd that the Arabic hero looks as Anglo as Tom Cruise while the equally Arabic villain has a hooked nose.
Advice: Own.

THE LION KING

The Basics: A young prince, believing he's responsible for the death of his father, exiles himself, regroups, and returns to claim his place as king of the jungle.
Nutshell Message: a) Remember who you are; b) Hakuna Matata (no worries).
Fun Fact: That's Mr. Bean (Rowen Atkinson) as Zazu.
Why to Watch: A true Disney original (okay, it does borrow from *Hamlet* a bit . . . and *The Odyssey*). Strong Elton John tunes—although,

once again, the bad-guy song ("Be Prepared") is kind of lame. Timon and Pumbaa up there with the *Jungle Book* crew in the pantheon of Disney sidekicks.

Why to Avoid: Some discomfort about the "ethnic" voices of the hyenas. Oh, and the brutal death of Mufasa. This film is to animated flatulence what *Blazing Saddles* is to live-action flatulence.

Advice: Own—although have the fast-forward button ready when the stampede starts.

POCAHONTAS

The Basics: Native American woman falls for European boy and helps avoid a bloody battle in the pre-revolutionary New World.

Nutshell Message: All living things are connected. Native Americans are cooler than Europeans. Even fact-based Disney films can get a boost from animated animal sidekicks.

Fun Fact: The Governor sound familiar? Same voice as *Beauty and the Beast*'s Cogsworth (David Ogen Stiers).

Why to Watch: An (admittedly fictionalized) piece of American history. A good Stephen Swartz score.

Why to Avoid: Low on the cuteness scale—under-sixers might not find much to enjoy. Preponderance of guns. And at some point you may have to explain that, when Pocahontas met John Smith, she was probably only ten or eleven years old.

Advice: Wait a few years.

THE HUNCHBACK OF NOTRE DAME

The basics: Deformed bellringer under the thumb of a crazed cleric (actually, for this version he's been changed from a minister to a minister of justice) yearns to be out there with the rest of the world. He falls for an oppressed gypsy who falls for another man.

Movies

Nutshell Messages: Cathedrals aren't sanctuaries for everyone. When it comes to the election of King of the Fools, it's who you know. Even those whose outward appearance ain't so conventionally attractive can have a lively inner life.

Fun Fact: You can spot Belle, from *Beauty and the Beast,* wandering through the crowd in the "Out There" musical sequence.

Why to Watch: Rich animation. Complex characters. "Out There" is a pretty good song. Esmeralda is . . . wait, that's not a good reason. Read on.

Why to Avoid: Perhaps the oddest choice ever for a Disney adaptation. Plus, Esmeralda is probably the most provocative Disney heroine ever (She's voiced by Demi Moore, who was in the movie *Striptease* that same year). Boy doesn't get girl. Talking statues are a desperation move to appeal to kids. If that's not all, let us site a bit of lyric song by Frollo: "Like fire/Hellfire/ This fire in my skin/This burning/ Desire/Is turning me to sin." It sure ain't "Bibbidi Bobbidy Boo."

Advice: Wait a while . . . maybe until after puberty.

HERCULES

The basics: A baby with superhuman strength finds out that his parents are gods and goes on a quest to get back into Mt. Olympus.

Nutshell Message: Anyone can be a hero. Gods can be a lot like us.

Fun Fact: In mythology, Hades is actually a pretty good guy, er, god. At least, he's not the demon we normally think him to be.

Why to Watch: Because in this case, the fact that it has almost nothing to do with the original Greek and Roman myths is a very good thing (to cite one example, animated Herc doesn't slaughter his wife and children).

Why to Avoid: A difficult-to-grasp expository opening ten minutes or so long. Lots of stuff about death (the villain, after all, is master of the underworld).
Advice: Push it back a few years.

MULAN

The basics: Young woman dresses as young man to become warrior in feudal China.
Nutshell message: Girl power.
Fun fact: *Mulan* is credited with launching the career of Christina Aguilera, who scored a hit with the song "Reflection."
Why to Watch: Because Mulan could kick the butt of any other Disney Princess—and half the Disney princes. Because it was a huge deal for Disney to be seriously looking at other cultures—and not just in a fairy tale kind of way. But unlike *Pocahontas*, which suffers from self-righteousness, *Mulan* is a terrific movie—even if

Eddie-Murphy-as-Mulan's-dragon seems like a mere audition for Eddie-Murphy-as-Shrek's-donkey.
Why to Avoid: Follow me on this one. Your kid is probably enlightened (or naïve) enough not to have ever considered the notion that women now or any time in the past were considered inferior and incapable. That's a good thing. But in order for the actions in Mulan to make sense, he or she has to understand that those biases have existed. So it's possible that by showing them *Mulan* at too early an age, you are actually planting that seed. Or maybe we're overthinking it. Need another reason? The epic battle scenes get pretty intense. And there's no Ratigan/Gaston playfulness about the villain, Shan-Yu, who is one of the vilest yet least memorable in Disney history.
Advice: Hold off a bit.

TARZAN

The basics: Orphan raised by monkeys meets fellow humans for the first time.

Nutshell Messages: All would be cool if we just left the animals alone. It's possible to have a musical where very few characters sing. Adoptive parents rock.

Fun Fact: Since the first one debuted in 1914, there has been at least one—and often many more than one—Tarzan film each decade.

Why to Watch: It's the last of the films in Disney's golden resurgence of musicals that began with *The Little Mermaid*. Some decent Phil Collins songs. Minnie Driver's animated counterpart is hotter than she is in real life. The opening sequence is actually powerful cinema.

Why to Avoid: That same opening sequence, in which T's parents are killed, is beautifully done and brief but damn intense, nonetheless. Rosie O'Donnell voices an ape annoyingly. Video-game-inspired tree-surfing scenes may encourage excess furniture climbing.

Advice: Wait.

FANTASIA *2000*

The basics: The original *Fantasia* "Sorcerer's Apprentice" sequence is combined with new animation, hosted by Yitzhak Perlman, Steve Martin and others.

Nutshell Message: Music is cool

Fun Fact: Disney's original plan for *Fantasia* was to update it every few years. Okay, so they were a little off schedule.

Why to Watch: It's spectacular on the IMAX screen it was intended for.

Why to Avoid: You don't have an IMAX screen in your house.

Advice: Whether or not you watch it, it's not a bad idea to play some classical music around the house once in a while.

THE EMPEROR'S NEW GROOVE

The basics: A self-absorbed emperor gets turned into a llama by his evil ex-advisor and sidekick in a rare thing for Disney: a nonmusical comedy. Think of it as an *Aladdin* without the songs.

Nutshell Message: Think about others before yourself.

Fun Fact: This could be one of the most altered-in-development productions in Disney history: it started as a Incan version of *The Prince and the Pauper* (under *Kingdom of the Sun* and other titles) with songs written by Sting.

Why to Watch: More laughs-per-minute than any Disney film ever.

Why to Avoid: You want more from Disney than laughs.

Advice: If it's a choice between this and an animated series on The Disney Channel, go ahead and watch this.

Verdict: Chill out and enjoy it.

ATLANTIS: THE LOST EMPIRE

The basics: Milo and a ragtag group of adventurers search for the lost city of Atlantis.

Nutshell message: Money isn't as important as saving a civilization.

Fun fact: A rare Disney film that has no anthropomorphic animals. Also, its direct-to-video sequel, *Atlantis: Milo's Return,* was cobbled together from three episodes of a proposed TV series that never aired—because the original film tanked.

Why to Watch: Because, for some unknown reason, your kids' two favorite Disney flicks are *Treasure Planet* and *The Black Cauldron.* Also, for the novelty of seeing a Disney character (Wilhelmina) smoking.

Why to Avoid: Because it was the second Disney animated film to be rated PG. Because a whole civilization is wiped out. Because its magical gobbledygoop about the magic of crystals is so eighties

Movies

(despite the movie being released in 2001)—and so lame—and so difficult to follow, even for adults. Because you hate the fact that Disney gave up on its feature musicals to produce stuff like this, which, come on, is there anyone at Disneyland right now clamoring to see Kida or The Mole? Is anyone going out this year for Halloween as Milo?

Advice: Skip it.

LILO AND STITCH

The basics: Hawaiian girl thinks alien Experiment 626 is a dog.

Nutshell Message: Ohana—basically, the idea that family transcends genes—and planets.

Fun Fact: *Lilo and Stitch* may well be the only Disney animated film that takes place in a world where Disney films are part of the culture. Play *I Spy* and watch for a *Mulan* poster and a Dumbo stuffed animal.

Why to Watch: Pick up a few Hawaiian words. Groovy

"Hawaiian Roller Coaster Ride" song. Credits appear ten minutes into the movie.

Why to Avoid: You don't want to deal with your preschooler imitating the annoying-voiced Stitch. The Disney Channel spinoff sucks. Lilo bites a kid.

Advice: Sure, why not?

TREASURE PLANET

The basics: Robert Louis Stevenson meets Isaac Asimov.

Nutshell Message: True treasure isn't gold, but friends and family are. Chart your own course.

Fun Fact: There aren't really pirates in space—and, if there were, our rudimentary memories of science class tell us that sails wouldn't be terribly useful in navigating a spaceship. We could be wrong.

Why to Watch: Some Disney excitement. A step up from *Atlantis*.

Why to Avoid: Because this is Disney pandering—an insult to kids, really. Back in the day,

Disney used to make live-action versions of great adventure books: *Treasure Island, 20,000 Leagues Under the Sea*, and the like. It trusted its audiences. Sure, they weren't always the most literal translations, but they weren't tarted up with robots and monsters and other "we need to appeal to today's young people" nonsense. Also, as with Atlantis, this is a case of Disney not having any idea what it's particularly good at. And all that might be forgiven if the emotional payoff worked, the story were exciting, and just about everything between the opening and the climax didn't feel like filler.

Advice: You've got plenty of other options.

BROTHER BEAR

The Basics: Eskimo boy kills bear, becomes bear, befriends bear who (spoiler alert) is son of the bear he killed, and learns that . . .

Nutshell Message: . . . you've got to see the world through other people's/creatures' eyes. Love is the most precious of totems. Oh, and never try to milk a caribou.

Fun Fact: The bantering caribou are played by Dave Thomas and Rick Moranis, best known as bantering beer-drinking Canadian brothers Doug and Bob McKenzie from *SCTV* and the movie *Strange Brew*.

Why to Watch: A well-written tale with solid characters, a fun musical number down by the swimming hole, and effective animation (and because your child didn't get upset at *Bambi* or *The Fox and the Hound*).

Why to Avoid: Because, man, does this get depressing. One lyric states, "There's no way out of this dark place," which is a far cry from "Whistle while you work." There are also a couple of nasty bear fights.

Advice: Wait a few years.

Movies

HOME ON
THE RANGE

The Basics: A group of cows try to save their farm.

Nutshell Message: Teamwork gets the job done. We all deserve a small piece of happiness.

Fun Fact: The last major Disney animated film released on VHS.

Why to Watch: Alan Mencken, of *Beauty and the Beast* and *The Little Mermaid* fame, returns to the Disney songwriting fold. Some fun attempts to steal some 1940s Warner Brothers animation thunder.

Why to Avoid: *Lilo and Stitch* showed that Disney can still be quirkily original. *Home on the Range* shows what happens when an animated film is more about referencing other films than carving out territory for itself. Side note: do we really need this many udder jokes in a kid flick? Aren't they, you know, nipples?

Advice: Skip.

We're going to stop here, because it's the last of the Disney traditional animated films. After *Home on the Range,* Disney shut down its Orlando and Paris studios. Would good stuff continue to come out under the Disney animation banner? Of course, but we've got other things to get to.

Disney Live Action to Watch/Avoid

The Mouse Factory is best known for its animation canon, but it has also generated reels and reels of live-action films without a cartoon mouse in sight. Some are good. Some are bad. Many star a young Kurt Russell. Here are a few that should be on your parental radar:

20,000 Leagues Under the Sea (1954). As good as Disney live action gets—and it's got an A-list cast including Kirk Douglas, Peter Lorre, and James Mason. Will your kid care? Probably not—at least until the giant squid attack. Avoid . . . for now.

Old Yeller (1957). The beloved dog turns vicious and has to be shot. Do we need to tell you anything more? Avoid.

The Shaggy Dog (1959). Now we're talking. As groundbreaking, in its own way, as *Snow White and the Seven Dwarfs* or *The Little Mermaid*, this wacky comedy opened the door to a parade of Disney films with really, really goofy premises. In this one, a kid (Tommy Kirk) turns into the titular dog. Mid-level hilarity ensues. Fred McMurray takes his place as the great American dad. Watch.

Darby O'Gill and the Little People (1959). A really terrific fantasy film that will probably bore your kids, who will get frustrated at the

Irish accents and by your attempts to explain who Sean Connery is. Avoid . . . for now.

Toby Tyler, or Ten Weeks With a Circus (1960). Another landmark in Disney cinema, this charming film about a boy who signs up with the big top is, as far as we know, the first Disney film where a monkey got major screen time. Monkeys rock. If *The Hours* or *The English Patient* had monkeys in them, we might have been able to sit through them. Watch.

The Absent Minded Professor (1961). Fred McMurray is back, this time as the inventor of the flying rubber called *flubber*. Robin Williams doesn't hold a candle to him. And the basketball game is a hoot. Watch.

The Parent Trap (1961). The Lindsey Lohan remake is actually better. Either way, though, you don't want to have to explain divorce or separation to your four-year-old. Avoid.

Babes in Toyland (1961). The whole thing comes off as a bad episode of *The Wonderful World of Disney* but your kids might actually enjoy this Mother Goose–inspired musical starring Annette Funicello as Mary Contrary and the ubiquitous Tommy Kirk as Tom Piper. Ray "Scarecrow" Bolger is the villain. Watch.

Polyanna (1960). She's so happy, they named a state of mind after her. Watch . . . but have insulin handy.

The Incredible Journey (1963). If you see this film before the 1993 remake *Homeward Bound: The Incredible Journey,* you might be okay. If you see it after, your kids are going to say, "Hey, why aren't the animals talking?" Watch.

Monkeys Go Home! (1967). A lesser-known Disney offering, but worth mentioning here because there are lots of monkeys in it. Dean Jones plays a guy who figures out how to use monkeys to pick olives. We're not kidding. Watch.

The One and Only, Original Family Band (1968). Think of it as an 1800s Partridge Family—assuming you remember the Partridge Family. Plus, it's got Kurt Russell. Watch.

The Love Bug (1969). When your kid has seen *Cars* a few too many times, try this one. Avoid the sequels and the remake. At the time, this was the second biggest grossing Disney film—after *Mary Poppins*. Watch.

The Barefoot Executive. (1971) Not for the younger kids, but we have to mention it here, not only because it's got Kurt Russell but because this story of a chimp that picks hit TV shows is one of this book's co-author's top twenty-five films of all time. Avoid . . . for now.

The World's Greatest Athlete (1973). No, it's not Kurt Russell starring in *The Michael Jordan Story* (although we'd pay to see that). This is the tale of a kid raised in the jungle who happens to run really fast. Why not? Watch.

The Apple Dumpling Gang (1975). You may have good memories of this Tim Conway/Don Knotts vehicle. You may not want to ruin them by watching . . . well, you know what? We're being too cynical. It's actually a good enough movie, and we wish we were living in a world where a movie called *The Apple Dumpling Gang* could actually get a theatrical release. Bravo, Conway! Viva, Knotts! Watch.

Freaky Friday (1977). Mom and daughter switch bodies. Both versions are good, but by renting the Jodi Foster original, you don't have to explain to your kids the sad saga of Lindsey Lohan. Watch . . . although your kids might lose interest.

Return to Oz (1985). We're in strange territory here. Great that the screenwriters pulled characters

Movies

from the actual L. Frank Baum Oz sequels. But it's difficult to get past the disturbing Kansas scenes without help from a "Somewhere Over the Rainbow"-ish song. In fact, kids who grew up on the Judy Garland original may have trouble with the lack of music, not to mention the drab colors and general somberness. Not surprisingly, it tanked. Avoid.

The Journey of Natty Gann (1985). Some underrated Disney greatness here, where a girl travels through the great picturesque outdoors—helped by John Cusack and a wolf—to find her dad. Happy ending helps considerably. Watch . . . even after your kid falls asleep.

Honey, I Shrunk the Kids (1989). Parents are pretty stupid. Kids are cool. And audiences are exposed to such mind-expanding concepts as "What would it be like to swim in a bowl of cereal?" Watch.

The Mighty Ducks (1992). It's a kids' hockey film. And it's better than *MVP: Most Valuable Primate* (as much as we love monkey movies). For little kids, it's also a lot more appropriate than *The Bad News Bears* or *The Sandlot*. As an intro to sports movie clichés, not a bad viewing experience with your sports-minded kid.

Hocus Pocus (1993). Bette Midler, Sarah Jessica Parker, and Kathy Nejinski? Najamini? whatever—play witches. We're pretty sure we're the only book that has mentioned this movie in the past fifteen years. Avoid.

The Santa Claus (1994). Tim Allen found life after *Home Improvement* through this and its sequels. Looked pretty good for a while there—until *Elf* came along and eclipsed it. Watch . . . but buy *Elf*.

101 Dalmatians (1996). Live-action version of the animated multidog flick was wildly popular and spawned a sequel. We're just glad it didn't spawn real-peopled versions of *The Aristocats* and *Lady and the Tramp*. Avoid.

George of the Jungle (1997). Live-action version of the cartoon that you probably don't remember. Pretty darn funny, especially by Disney live-action standards. Watch.

Air Bud (1997). Dog plays football. Or was it basketball? That's right, it was basketball. In the sequel it was football. Or was that *Free Willy*? Did the whale play football? No, couldn't be. Definitely was basketball. And a dog. Watch.

Inspector Gadget (1999). Okay, who placed the order on this one? Matthew Broderick plays a robot-ish guy who . . . oh, never mind. While you still have control over your remote control, stay away from generic junk like this. Avoid.

The Princess Diaries (2001). Sweet stuff about an American nerd who is really a princess. Dad has probably already found the Internet site that shows the actress in a topless scene in another film. Just thought we should put that out there. Watch.

The Country Bears (2002). In hindsight, think of this—and *Haunted Mansion*—as what Disney had to clear its throat with in order to get the amusement-park-ride-turned-movie right with *Pirates of the Caribbean*. Avoid.

Sky High (2005). If there weren't four thousand other films about the real lives of superheroes, this would be hailed as a masterpiece. As it is, it's good—although . . . avoid. Since the fights are big and the flame-throwing villain pretty intense, you are best off keeping it out of your queue for now.

Movies

You've Got Animation in My Live Action/You've Got Live Action in My Animation

In the Disney world and occasionally elsewhere, you'll find hybrid films—flicks where some sequences are animated and some are live action. There are many potential pitfalls to this approach.

Moviemaking is a time-consuming business. Animated movies even more so. When you are dealing with a timeless project like *Cinderella* or *Pinocchio*, it really doesn't matter if your film comes out in 1939 or 1943 or whenever.

But if your live-action is star-driven, you run what we call *The Pagemaster* Risk. By the time that expensive obscurity hit theaters, star Macauley Culkin was no longer the Hollywood "it" guy he was when he signed the contract. A similar fate hit *Space Jam*, which instantly became dated because it assumes that kids will always know and care about Michael Jordan.

The other risk is that a studio casts its live action with an eye toward broadening the possible demographic and, in doing so, scares away the core audience. What genius decided that Bill

Murray and Chris Elliot should carry the live-action burden of *Osmosis Jones?* And as much as it was praised at the time, you'll find few tyke fans of *Who Framed Roger Rabbit?*, a film too frantic in its animation and too dark and convoluted in its live action to hold up beyond the initial hype. And don't even get us started on the casting of Robert De Niro and Jason Alexander in *The Adventures of Rocky and Bullwinkle* (a project with problems that go well beyond the casting).

When does it work? Primarily when the film is set in a period other than the present. *Mary Poppins, Bedknobs and Broomsticks,* and, to a lesser extent, *Pete's Dragon* are films likely to entertain the kids and grandkids of their original audiences. And while contemporary, odds are good that the genre-mocking *Enchanted*—with a fun score and charming lead—will be a perennial hit for Disney (although younger kids are likely to dig the animated opening much more than the rest of the film).

Difficult to objectively judge, or even see, these days is *Song of the South,* a movie that is best known now strictly for its animation-meets-live-action song sequences featuring James Baskett as Uncle Remus. The rest of the film has had a tumultuous history because its detractors believe that it trivializes slavery—a thought that could certainly sour your zippety-do-da day.

Pixar Sticks

With all due respect to the giant green ogres, shark mobsters, furry zoo inhabitants, celebrity-voiced bees, and other assorted computer-generated characters that nowadays seem to find their way onto the big screen on a monthly basis, almost without exception the best computer-generated movies of recent years—scratch that—the best movies of recent years, period—are the ones created by Pixar Animation Studios (now owned by the Walt Disney Company).

If we had to venture a guess, we suspect you probably already know that. Unlike your father's animated films (or, put another way, the films you grew up watching) Pixar's winning cinematic roster appeals as much to adults as it does children.

And since we're going out on a limb by assuming that none of this is news to you, we're not going to spill a lot of ink (this stuff ain't cheap) on reminding you of something you already know. Rather, we're simply going to evoke the names of these films. Meditate on them, smile, and anxiously look forward to the next one.

Toy Story
A Bug's Life
Toy Story 2
Monsters, Inc.
Finding Nemo
The Incredibles
Cars
Ratatouille

Hey, What's He / She Doing in a Kid Flick?

Here are ten performers who you'd never think would appear in a movie being watched by your five-year-old:

1. **Joe Mantegna** *(Baby's Day Out)*
2. **Christopher Walken** *(Kangaroo Jack)*
3. **Robert De Niro** *(The Adventures of Rocky and Bullwinkle)*
4. **Peter Fonda** *(Thomas and the Magic Railroad)*
5. **Sandra Bernhard** *(Sesame Street Presents: Follow That Bird)*
6. **Kathy Griffin** *(Muppets from Space)*
7. **Michael Jackson** *(The Wiz)*
8. **Jon Voight** *(Holes)*
9. **Harvey Keitel** *(Monkey Trouble)*
10. **Kathleen Turner** *(A Simple Wish)*

Movies

The Other Guys:
The Best of Non-Disney
Traditional Animation
Feature Films

For years, Disney monopolized the world of feature film animation. But occasionally, a challenger comes along . . . and even more occasionally, it's a film worth your eighty-two minutes (or thereabouts).

Here's a short list of the ones worth a look. And a slightly longer list of ones that you should wait on or ignore completely.

WORTH THE TIME

The Swan Princess. The most Disneylike of the animated competitors, this tale opens with the "I want" song, features a big gimmick song, a villain number, etc. And it tells it well. Singer Liz Callaway offers terrific voice to the title heroine.

The Secret of NIMH. Awkward title but smart, exciting flick. At the risk of giving away part of the title secret, we will tell you that NIMH stands for the National Institute of Mental Health.

The Land Before Time. Dinosaur flick that spawned a seemingly endless series of straight-to-video sequels (plus an unofficial ripoff remake in Disney's *Dinosaur*). The original is a charmer, with characters kids can relate to, positive messages about appreciating differences, and a reasonably scary T-rex around to keep things interesting.

An American Tail. A well-done look at the immigrant experience—through the eyes of a young Jewish mouse. This is the rare non-Disney cartoon that spawned a popular song ("Somewhere Out There").

Curious George. Gentle take on the pesky monkey's story. A great pop score helps up the rewatch factor considerably.

Charlotte's Web. The style may be a little dated and the sadness quotient a bit high, but this is a great story with winning characters—including Paul Lynde as Templeton the Rat, Debbie Reynolds as Charlotte, and Henry Gibson as Wilbur.

BEST TO WAIT

Anastasia. Nicely done—but is your kid really ready for a dose of Russian history?

The Prince of Egypt. Nicely done—but is your kid really ready for the plagues?

The Iron Giant. Nicely done—but is your kid really ready to sob his eyes out at the end—and watch you do the same?

Anything by Hayao Miyazaki, creator of such wonders as *Spirited Away, Howl's Moving Castle,* and *Kiki's Delivery Service.*

Movies

Ten Movies To Know That We Couldn't Fit in Anywhere Else

1 *The Neverending Story.* An exciting adventure filled with wonderful characters—your kid is likely to want his own luck dragon. Ah, if that could be so . . . . Be ready for an emotional reaction, though, when the hero's trusty horse is slipping into the yucky swamp.

2 *Willy Wonka and the Chocolate Factory.* Yes, we know, there was a remake. But we're going to focus on the original, which takes its time in the beginning, setting up the wonderful relationship between Charlie and his Grandpa Joe before setting them loose in the memorably detailed workplace.

3 *The Little Rascals.* If this attempt to resuscitate the legendary series from the 1920s–40s were just a hair better written, it might have spawned a long series of sequels. As it stands, though, this is a fun look at a group of young boys getting into scrapes, learning about friendship, and learning that girls aren't so bad. You and your kid will wish you lived in a neighborhood where more people played in their front yards instead of the back ones.

4 *The Black Stallion/National Velvet* et. al. Very soon, your child may love horses. Right now, though, they are big, scary animals. Wait a bit before playing these classics.

5 *Madeline.* An understated masterpiece that captures the spirit of the original books while expanding the stories in a way that doesn't compromise the overall integrity of the books. A group of orphans in Paris make life interesting for their supervisory nun (a knowing Frances McDormand). You'll want to adopt every one of them.

6 *Annie.* A bloated attempt to bring the Broadway hit to the big screen. The made-for-TV Disney version is less cinematic but much more entertaining.

7 *Over the Hedge.* Great characters make all the difference in an animated film. Here, a motley group of beasts try to infiltrate a suburban neighborhood. And despite overexaggerated missteps, the whole thing works remarkably well. Unfortunately, with a glut of computer-animated films, it didn't really stake out any new territory and thus isn't particularly well remembered.

8 *Wallace and Gromit: The Curse of the Were-rabbit.* The W&G films are painstakingly admirable but—and we may be heretical in saying this—not ever as fun as we hope they'll be. We think your kid will feel the same way.

9 *The Brave Little Toaster.* All we're saying—and this is all we're going to say—is that this is an animated film in which all the major characters are appliances. Appliances. Oh, we'll say one other thing: it's actually a charming, exciting movie. But there's no getting around the fact that it's about appliances.

10 *Monsters, Inc.* It's amazing how a credit sequence can get you in the mood for a film. Think *West Side Story.* Think *Catch Me If You Can.* And think this star in the Pixar hit parade. The rest of the movie—about a pair of monsters dealing with a little girl who accidentally ended up in their world—is just as fun.

Part V

CHARACTERS, CHARACTERS EVERYWHERE

Now that we've covered all the major kid-focused mass media, let's look at a wide range of other sources of kid culture. We're talking about theater, about arena shows, about board games, about breakfast cereals, and about theme parks.

Theater: *Annie*, et al

There's nothing like a live theater production. We're not saying that's necessarily good or necessarily bad, but trust us, there's nothing like it.

On the one hand, there's something immediate and intimate about seeing real actors on stage. On the other hand, there's something equally real and intimate about spending $100 for two tickets to a show, only to spend the whole time in the lobby because your talkative kid won't shut up.

Now, there are outstanding children's theaters around the country. There are also rank amateur theaters that treat the junior market as a cash cow that requires little creative effort.

What follows are some of the main-stage shows you may be tempted to take your preschoolers to, along with some caveats. But first, some nuggets of wisdom:

1. As much as it sucks to waste the ticket money, if your kid is disruptive, you must retreat to the lobby. You've got no right to ruin anyone else's good time (of course, good time is a relative term when it comes to a community theater production of *The Music Man*).

2. If it's a musical (and what business do you have taking a kid to a show if it's not a musical?), you'd be well-advised to play the cast recording in the car for a week or two before going. That anticipation of the next song could be a big factor in keeping him in the theater for the entire show.

3. Have candy on hand to bribe silence. *Don't* give your kid the bag. You don't want her self-medicating here, lest the bag be gone well before intermission. And where does that leave you?

4. Speaking of candy, lean toward treats that have a long processing time. A lollypop will hold off problems longer than a bag of Skittles.

5. Don't tell your kid not to talk and then continually whisper, "Do you like it?" "Did you see that?" etc. In other words, shut your trap.

6. If it's going to be your first time taking your kid to a show, try to get aisle seats.

With all that in mind, here are the highs and lows of some popular gateway shows that parents use to introduce their kids to non-children's-theater theater:

Annie. If it's a community theater production, expect to see an army of orphans on stage. When a company doesn't have to pay its actors, it can overload the play with the full knowledge that each kid will attract ticket-buying parents, grandparents, aunts, uncles, etc.– even if she's just lip-synching to "It's the Hard-Knock Life."

Beauty and the Beast. There are many versions of this classic tale. If you want to ensure that what you are seeing has "Be Our Guest" and other familiar songs in it, make sure that what you are to attend has the title of *Disney's Beauty and the Beast.*

Joseph and the Amazing Technicolor Dreamcoat. Andrew Lloyd Webber does the Bible again, but with a much more whimsical touch than with *Jesus Christ Superstar.* (We all know how that story ends.) The pluses here are nonstop music, an upbeat ending, and plenty of opportunities for silliness. The

Characters

downside? "Dad, did those guys really sell their brother? Will my brothers ever sell me?"

The Lion King. Rather than being based on a classic story, *The Lion King* is purely a Disney creation. Therefore, any production for the foreseeable future will be the Julie Taymor–directed Broadway version. Which means you are paying top dollar to sit in the lobby if your kid has trouble with the trampling death of Mufasa.

Once Upon a Mattress. This enduring musical adaptation of *The Princess and the Pea* has a good rep as a kid show–and is likely to surprise parents with its subplot involving a knight who discovers that his girlfriend is pregnant.

Seussical. Much more popular in regional theaters than it was on Broadway, this musical combines some of the most familiar Dr. Seuss stories into one fairly confusing plot. The core story, though, of Horton the elephant and a Who kid named JoJo is charming. And there are some better than average songs. Careful of the Wickersham Brothers, though. These monkey siblings who torment Horton can be creepy.

The Sound of Music. You may pick up tickets because you remember "Do-Re-Mi" and the goat puppets. Do we need to remind you of the villains of the piece? Prepare yourself for, "Mom, what's a Nazi?"

The Wiz. This underrated musical is a great introduction to grown-up theater, especially if your kids already are familiar with the Wizard of Oz story. Just don't prepare them by screening the messy film version that tries to pass off a thirty-plus-year-old Diana Ross as Dorothy.

Arena Shows:
Better Skate Than Never

Not quite a theater production or dance recital and not quite an athletic event, the ice show—and its cousin, the nonskating arena show—may well be your child's first exposure to mass market live entertainment.

We're not going to get all preachy and tell you how artistically lame *Rugrats: Live and in Diapers* or *Playhouse Disney Live! On Tour* are. We won't presume you were expecting Ibsen. We understand the main reasons why parents flock to these things.

1 The tickets are usually relatively inexpensive and the shows usually stay comfortably within the hour-and-a-half mark.

2 The characters are very familiar, so there's little risk of your kid absolutely hating it.

3 These usually are staged in facilities devoted to basketball games and major rock concerts. Therefore, your yappy kid is likely to be among other yappy kids. And you are less likely to get icy stares from the parents of the well-behaved tykes.

We will warn you, though, that while it's relatively easy to dodge the tiny shopping area at theater productions, it's nearly impossible to avoid buying the junk being hawked in the aisles at these things. Just prepare for it. And know that, when you walk in the doors of the arena, there's most likely a light-up stick in your future.

Characters

Chance Encounters: Board Games, Your Kid, and You

We know it's a little off-topic, yet we can't help but put in a plug here for that staple of interactive entertainment: the board game. Long before kids were jumping on mushrooms in Super Mario Brothers or gunning down pimps in Grand Theft Auto, they were visiting the land of Queen Frostine in Candyland and winning second prize in a beauty pageant, courtesy of the Monopoly moneybags dude.

While we're not going to debate the merits and demerits of computer games, we are going to encourage supplementing them with their low-tech cousins such as Sorry, Parcheesi, and Trouble. What you'll soon realize—but you'll want to keep from your kid—is that Clue is teaching deductive reasoning, Perfection is improving their special relations, and Monopoly is covering basic math skills (as long as you aren't playing the horrifying credit-card-using newer edition. Don't even get us started on that bastardization of a great thing).

More importantly, by playing games, you are sending the message that your kid is worth spending time with, that parents and kids can have fun together, and that what they are enjoying truly matters.

And if you need another excuse for having lots of games around the house, consider this: most of them can be adapted (after the kids are asleep, of course), into fun drinking games. Shots and Ladders, anyone?

Breakfast Cereal: Your Sugar-pushing Friends

Some characters your children encounter have little or nothing to do with books, movies, TV, or music. But they have everything to do with breakfast.

We're talking about Toucan Sam, Sugar Bear, Dig 'em Frog, Snap, Krackle, and Pop, and all their kid cereal brethren. Yes, we know this gang was born in the imagination of marketers trying to convince kids that sugar cereal is part of a balanced breakfast, but that doesn't make them any less real in the pop culture life of your family.

Given how all pervasive they are, it's amazing how little we know about them. For instance, can you name any of Cap'n Crunch's crew? Who was ruler before King Vitamin ascended to the throne? And whatever happened to Quisp and Quake?

What we do know is that an awful lot of thievery goes on in commercials for these products, whether it's those crossover

Characters

Flintstones trying to abscond with Fruity Pebbles or the Trix rabbit perpetrating some corn-byproduct-induced felony or L.C. Leprechaun, with his oft-mocked Irish accent, claiming divine right on the purple moons and green clovers of Lucky Charms by virtue of their magical deliciosity. So the message is not exactly a positive one.

Why, then, do these cereal characters loom in our consciousness? And why should we expect them to do the same in our children?

Because the marketers know what they are doing, that's why. And because most of these cereals taste, well, "Grrrrrrrrrrreat!"—at least, a lot better than than boring, healthy crap in the prize-free boxes.

Live: Look Honey, It's the Real Mickey!

When you are under five years old and at DisneyWorld, Disneyland, or any other character-heavy theme park, the most exciting part of the day isn't the rides. It's seeing your favorite characters, giving a hug, posing for a picture, and maybe scoring an autograph. Tikes approach these costumed creatures with reactions ranging from blind fear to rock-fan enthusiasm. How can you best prepare your kid for the big moment? Here are some tips:

1. Have an excuse ready as to why Winnie the Pooh refuses to talk. When they get people-sized, you might say, they lose their voice boxes. It seems like a fair trade.

Another possibility is to suggest that Ursula the sea witch is behind it all. Or you can just say it's part of their union contract.

2. Have an excuse ready for the issues of proportion that are likely to come up. Why, for instance, are Cinderella's mice just as big as Cinderella? The under-five set should be content with "So you won't step on them."

3. Don't expect to serendipitously find your kid's favorites. Yes, it's fun to randomly run into characters throughout the park. But the ones you randomly run into are more likely to be obscurities, such as King John from *Robin Hood*, as they are to be a major princess or a gold-plated cartoon character. These stars are more likely to make scheduled appearances at appointed times.

4. No matter how much your child went on and on about sitting with, say, Ariel, if you get to the moment of truth and he pulls a tearful about-face, go with it. Forcing your kid onto the lap of a woman in a sweaty suit isn't good for anyone. And the picture you snap is going to be awful.

5. You are dedicating your day to your kids' enjoyment. Therefore, don't feel guilty if you take a few minutes to admire the attributes of one of the princes or princess. (Assuming the actor or actress is unquestionably of age, of course.)

6. We once witnessed Tweedledum (or maybe it was Tweedledee) falling backwards over a hedge, requiring assistance to extricate himself. It was truly one of the funniest things we've ever seen. That being said, you shouldn't allow your troublemaking kid to recreate such a moment. Pulling a character's tail, pinching, tripping, etc. should be stopped—as hilarious as the end results might be.

Afterword

Okay, here come the clichés:

* Your kids are only young once. Enjoy them.

* You chose to bring your kids into the world. Prioritize them.

* All the movies, TV shows, computer games, and other distractions in the world can't make up for you not spending time with your kids.

* We live in a complicated world. You are going to make parental mistakes. But kids are remarkably resilient. Give yourself a break.

* Kids are among the most fun people on the planet. Try to realize that every day.

Quiz Answers

Wait, You Didn't Say This Book Was Going to Be on the Test

1)
a. *Chicka Chicka Boom Boom*
b. *Brown Bear, Brown Bear, What Do You See?*
c. *The Saggy, Baggy Elephant*
d. *Richard Scarry's Best Storybook Ever.*
e. *Blueberries for Sal.*

2) c. Unbearable

3) Swamp

4) c. Oliver Hardy

5) *Jumanji*

6)
Amy Tan
The Joy Luck Club (a)
The Moon Lady (c)

John Updike
Rabbit Run (a)
A Child's Calendar (c)

Joyce Carol Oates
Big Mouth & Ugly Girl (c)
Where Are You Going, Where Have You Been? (a)

Maya Angelou
My Painted House, My Friendly Chicken, and Me (c)
Even the Stars Look Lonesome (a)

7) Frog

8) Cookie.

9) Mulligan

10) Bull

11) They are tiny

12) A teddy bear

13) Put her finger in her mother's ring

14) Very nice guy

Sesame Test

1) b. 1969

2) a. Golden Condor

3) d. "Rubber Ducky"

4) Match the character to its favorite thing
Trash (Oscar)
Triangles (Telly Monster)
Baths (Ernie)
Cookies (Cookie Monster)
Pigeons (Bert)
Pet Rock (Zoe)

5) True

6) b. Gina

7) "A la peanut butter sandwiches."

8) c. 1996

9) Proprietor of The Mail it
Shop/Luis
Veterinarian/Gina
Music teacher/Bob
Science teacher/Gordon
Nurse/Susan

10) 8'2"

11) b. Super Grover

12) True

13) a. Maria

14) c. "It's a Wonderful Life"

15) a. 3

16) d. Cookie Monster

17) "where the air is sweet."

18) False. Originally orange

19) d. Rubber bands

20) c. Coat

21) a. Game show host

22) False. He does not own a dog.

23) d. Zoe

24) Billy Idol

25) False. He joined the show in 1984

The Songs Remain the Same

1) c. Up and down, and

d. Front and back

2) d. A round

3) "Bippity Boppity Boo"

4) A monkey and a weasel

5) b. Jump for joy

6) a. Short and stout

7) b. because

8) True

9) a. Climb up the spout again

10) "Twinkle Twinkle Little Star." "Baa Baa Black Sheep."

11) d. A nurse

12) 6

13) "There goes John Jacob Jingleheimer Schmidt."

14) False.

15) "Why, Mary loves the lamb, you know."

The Disney Princesses Quiz

1) Snow White; Cinderella;
Aurora; Ariel; Belle; Jasmine;
Pocahontas; Mulan

2) b. Belle

3) a. Mulan

4) d. Mulan

5) False

6) d. Aurora

7) Tiger (Jasmine)
Horse (Mulan)
Hummingbird (Pocahontas)
Mice (Cinderella)
Fish (Ariel)

8) c. Maurice

9) Jasmine

10) a. Flora, Fauna and
Merryweather

11) b. Pochantas and Mulan

12) c. Ariel

13) d. Pocahantas

14) False

15) c. Ariel

16) a. Jasmine

17) d. All of them

18) False: Jasmine

19) d. Pocahontas

20) "I want adventure in the great
wide somewhere/I want it more
than I can tell" (Belle)

"Up where they walk/Up where
they run/Up where they stay all
day in the sun" (Ariel)

"No matter how your heart is grieving/if you keep on believing/the dream that you wish will come true" (Cinderella)

"Some day when spring is here/We'll find our love anew/And the birds will sing/And wedding bells will ring" (Snow White)

"And I know it's true that visions are seldom all they seem/But if I know you, I know what you do/You love me at once, the way you did once upon a dream." (Aurora)

21) c. Aurora

22) c. Mulan

23) False

24) Pink

25) b. Jasmine

Your score: If you bothered to answer any of these questions at all, give yourself a big A+. You are one dedicated parent.
Now, go hug your kid.

Index

A

The Absent Minded Professor, 166

The Adventures of Harold and the
Purple Crayon, 16–17

The Adventures of Ichabod and
Mr. Toad, 137

The Adventures of Pinocchio, 13–14

The Adventures of Rocky and
Bullwinkle, 171, 173

Air Bud, 169

Aladdin, 156

Alexander, Jason, 34

Alice in Wonderland, 138

"Alouette," 120

"The Alphabet Song, " 120

America, 105

An American Tail, 175

Anastasia, 175

Anderson, Hans Christian, 14–15

And to Think I Saw It on Mulberry
Street, 91

Angela's Airplane, 49

Angelou, Maya, 29

Annie, 177, 181

Another Monster at the End of This
Book, 32

The Apple Dumpling Gang, 167

arena shows, 183

The Aristocats, 148

Arkin, Alan, 35

Armstrong, Louis, 104

The Art of Maurice Sendak, 24–25

Arthur, 62

Atlantis: The Lost Empire, 161–62

B

Babes in Toyland, 166

Baby's Day Out, 173

Bambi, 133–34

Barber, Ronde, 34

Barber, Tiki, 34

The Barefoot Executive, 167

Barney and Friends, 74–77

A Barnstormer in Oz, 57

The Barnyard Dance, 21

Batholomew and the Oobleck, 30

Batman, 78–79

Baum, L. Frank, 53–55

The Bear in the Big Blue House, 74–77

"The Bear Went Over the Mountain,"
120

The Beatles, 105, 114–15

Beauty and the Beast, 155–56, 181

Bedknobs and Broomsticks, 171

Bee Movie: The Honey Disaster, 48

Bemelmans, Ludwig, 17

Berenstain Bears, 46–47

Bernhard, Sandra, 173

The Best Way to Play, 38–39

"Bibbidi-Bobbidi-Boo," 104

Big Bad Voodoo Daddy, 101–2

"Bingo," 120

The Black Cauldron, 152

The Black Stallion, 176

Blackberry Subway Jam, 49
Blind Melon, 101
Blue's Clues, 83–84
board books, 20–21
board games, 184
Bob the Builder, 62–63
Boone, Debbie, 35
The Borrowers, 29
A Boy Named Charlie Brown, 123–24
The Brady Bunch, 90
Bragg, Billy, 103
The Brave Little Toaster, 177
breakfast cereal, 185–86
Bridwell, Norman, 47
Brooks, Mel, 34
Brother Bear, 163
Brown, Charlie, 121–25
Brown, Jeff, 51
Brown, Margaret Wise, 22
Brown, Mark, 62
Browne, Jackson, 57
A Bug's Life, 172
Burningham, John, 29
Burns, Steve, 83–84
Burton, LeVar, 68
The Butter Battle Book, 93
"Butterfly Kisses," 116

C

Caillou, 63
Candyland, 184
Cannon, Janell, 50
Carle, Eric, 35
The Carrot Seed, 21
Cars, 172
The Cat in the Hat, 91–94
"Cat's in the Cradle," 116
celebrity authors, 33–40
Celeste Sails to Spain, 50

characters at theme parks, 186–87
A Charlie Brown Christmas, 122
A Charlie Brown Thanksgiving, 124
Charlotte's Web, 175
Choo Choo Soul, 99
Cinderella, 12–13, 137–38
"The Circle Game," 105
Clifford the Big Red Dog, 46–47
Clive Eats Alligators, 50
Clue, 184
Coldplay, 105
Cole, Henry, 37
Collins, David, 69
Collodi, Carlo, 13–14
Colvin, Shawn, 61, 102
Cool J, L. L., 104
Cornell, Laura, 39
The Cosby Show, 39
Cosby, Bill, 36, 38–39, 89
Cosgrove, Rachel, 55
Counting Blessings, 35
The Country Bears, 169
Crystal, Billy, 34
Curious George, 19, 175
Curtis, Jamie Lee, 36, 39–40
Cyrus, Billy Ray, 117
Cyrus, Miley, 117

D

Daddy Makes the Best Spaghetti, 49
"Daddy's Little Girl," 116
Daisy-Head Mayzie, 31
Daltry, Roger, 57
Darby O'Gill and the Little People,
    165–66
The Dark Crystal, 60
The Dark Knight Returns, 78
Davey and Goliath, 81–82
A Day with Wilbur Robinson, 52

"Daydream Believer," 105
De Niro, Robert, 173
Denslow, W. W., 53
Denver, John, 61
Desputeaux, Helene, 63
*Dinosaur Bob and His Adventures
    with the Family Lazardo*, 52
Disney movies, 127, 130–69
Disneyland, 186
DisneyWorld, 186
"Do You Believe in Magic?," 105
"Don't Worry Be Happy," 105
Donovan, 105
The Doobie Brothers, 100–101
The Doodlebops, 99
Dora the Explorer, 63
Dorothy and the Wizard in Oz, 54
Dorough, Bob, 119
Double Trouble, 104
Dumbo, 132–33
Dundas, Shane, 69

E

Eastman, P. D., 51
The Electric Company, 39, 87
Elmopalooza, 61
Elmo Saves Christmas, 37
The Emerald City of Oz, 54
The Emperor's New Groove, 161
Enchanted, 171
Even More Flanimals, 35
Eywood, Varnette Hon, 39

F

Falwell, Jerry, 68, 74
Fantasia, 132
Fantasia 2000, 160
Farmer, Philip Jose, 57
Fat Albert and the Cosby Kids, 39, 89

"Father and Son," 116–17
"Feeling Groovy," 105
Fierstein, Harvey, 37
Finding Nemo, 172
The 5,000 Fingers of Dr. T, 92
Flanimals, 35
Flat Stanley, 51
Fleischer, Dave, 80
Fleischer, Max, 80
Folds, Ben, 117
Fonda, Peter, 173
The Fox and the Hound, 151
Franklin, 64
Freaky Friday, 167
Freeman, Morgan, 87
Freight Train, 20
Fugees, 103
Full House, 89–90
Fun and Fancy Free, 135–36

G

Garcia, Jerry, 100
Garland, Judy, 56
Geisel, Theodore, 91
George of the Jungle, 169
George Shrinks, 52
Gerald McBoing-Boing, 92
Gervais, Ricky, 35
Glinda of Oz, 55
Go, Diego, Go, 64
Go, Dog, Go, 51
Goldberg, Whoopi, 35
"Good Morning Starshine," 105
Goodnight Gorilla, 21
Goodnight Moon, 21–24
The Good Night Show, 84–85
"Gracie," 117
Grandma Gets Grumpy, 49
The Great Mouse Detective, 153

Green Eggs and Ham, 93
Griffin, Kathy, 173
Grimm Brothers, 12
Grisman, David, 100
Grover, 32–33
Grover and the Everything in the Whole Wide World Museum, 32, 61
Guaraldi, Vince, 123
Guess How Much I Love You, 20

H

H.R. Pufnstuf, 87–88
Halloween, 34
Happiness is a Warm Puppy, 122
"Happiness Runs," 105
Hardy, Oliver, 55
Henson, Jim, 60
Hercules, 158–59
Higglytown Heroes, 64–65
Hines, Anna Grossnickle, 49
His Majesty, The Scarecrow of Oz, 55
Hocus Pocus, 168
"Holes in the Floor of Heaven," 117
Holes, 173
Home on the Range, 164
Honey, I Shrunk the Kids, 168
Hooray for Diffendoofer Day, 31
Hop on Pop, 93
Horton Hatches the Egg, 91
Horton Hears a Who, 92, 95
How the Grinch Stole Christmas, 92–95
Howdy Doody, 87
Howl's Moving Castle, 175
The Hunchback of Notre Dame, 157–58

I

"I Don't Want to Live on the Moon," 102
I Love You Forever, 49
I'm a Manatee, 38
I Spy, 41
"I Wanna Be Like You," 101–2
ice shows, 183
The Imagination Movers, 99
The Incredibles, 172
In Search of Dr. Seuss, 94
In the Night Kitchen, 28
The Incredible Journey, 166
Inspector Gadget, 169
The Iron Giant, 175
It's a Big, Big World, 65
It's the Great Pumpkin, Charlie Brown, 123

J

Jackson, Michael, 56–57, 173
Jag's New Friend, 34
Joel, Billy, 35
"John Lee Supertaster," 103
Johnny and the Sprites, 65, 99
Johnson, Crockett, 16
Joseph and the Amazing Technicolor Dreamcoat, 181–82
Journey Back to Oz, 56
Journey of Natty Gann, 168
Joyce, William, 52
Jumanji, 28
The Jungle Book, 143
"Just Happy to Be Me," 103

K

Kamakawiwo'ole, Israel, 103–4
Kangaroo Jack, 173
Katrina and the Waves, 105

Keats, Ezra Jack, 49
Keitel, Harvey, 173
Kenny the Shark, 65–66
Kiki's Delivery Service, 175
Krofft, Marty, 87–88
Krofft, Sid, 87–88
Kunhardt, Dorothy, 19

L

Lady and the Tramp, 139–40
The Land Before Time, 175
Land of the Lost, 88
LazyTown, 66
The Leaf Men, 52
Lee, Spike, 35
Lee, Tonya, 35
The Lemming Condition, 35
Lepe, Michele, 85
Lester, Allison, 50
L'Heureux, Christine, 63
Lilo and Stitch, 162
The Lion King, 156–57, 182
Lipton, Leonard, 109
Lithgow, John, 36, 38
Little Bill, 39
Little Critter, 46–47
Little Einsteins, 64
The Little Engine that Could, 18–19
The Little Mermaid, 14–15, 154
The Little Rascals, 176
The Little Wizard Series, 55
"Lizard Lips and Chicken Hips," 101
The Lorax, 93
The Love Bug, 167
The Lovin' Spoonful, 105
Lowrey, Janette Sebring, 18
Lucas, George, 79

M

Madeline, 17, 177
Madonna, 33
The Magic School Bus, 89
Maguire, Gregory, 57
Mahalia Mouse Goes to College, 38
Make Mine Music, 135
Mantegna, Joe, 173
The Many Adventures of Winnie the Pooh, 149–50
Marsupial Sue, 38
Martinez, Melanie, 84–85
Martino, Al, 116
The Marvelous Land of Oz, 53
"Mary Had a Little Lamb," 104
Mary Poppins, 171
Math Curse, 46
Mathieu, Joe, 32
Max and Ruby, 66
McCall, David, 118
McDonald, Michael, 101
McElligot's Pool, 91
McFerrin, Bobby, 105
McGraw, Tim, 116
The Meanest Thing to Say, 39
Meet the Robinsons, 52
Melody Time, 136
MetLife, 125
The Mighty Ducks, 168
Miller, Frank, 78
Minnelli, Liza, 56
Miss Nelson is Missing, 28
Mitchell, Joni, 105
The Mitten, 21
Miyazaki, Hayao, 175
The Monkees, 105
Monkey Trouble, 173
Monkeys Go Home!, 166–67
Monopoly, 184

The Monster at the End of This Book, 32
Monsters, Inc., 172, 177
Moran, Sam, 86
Moreno, Rita, 87
Motion Picture Association of America, 129
movie ratings, 128–29
Mr. Rogers' Neighborhood, 90
Mulan, 37, 159
Munsch, Robert, 49
Muppets, 60–61
The Muppet Movie, 61
The Muppet Show, 60–61
Muppets from Space, 86, 173
"My Bonny Lies Over the Ocean," 120
"My Flying Saucer," 103

N
The Napping House, 21
Nash, Ogden, 109
National Velvet, 176
Neill, John R., 53–55
Nelson, Willie, 102–3
The Neverending Story, 176
New York State of Mind, 35
Noggin', 66–67
noisy books, 42–43
Nolan, Christopher, 78
Norville, Deborah, 36
Numeroff, Laura, 29

O
Oates, Joyce Carol, 29
Oh the Places You'll Go, 93
"Old McDonald Had a Farm, " 120
Old Yeller, 165
Oliver & Company, 153–54
Olsen, Ashley, 89–90

Olsen, Mary Kate, 89–90
Once Upon a Mattress, 182
The One and Only, Original Family Band, 167
101 Dalmatians, 141–42, 168–69
Ooh & Aah, 67
Osmosis Jones, 171
Over the Hedge, 177
The Oz Squad, 57
Ozma of Oz, 54

P
Page, Greg, 86
The Pagemaster, 170
The Paper Bag Princess, 49
Parcheesi, 184
The Parent Trap, 166
Pat the Bunny, 19, 29
The Patchwork Girl of Oz, 55
Patton, Donovan, 84
Payne, C. F., 38
Peanuts, 121–25
Perfection, 184
The Perhappsy Chaps, 55
Peter Pan, 138–39
Peter, Paul, and Mary, 109
Pete's Dragon, 171
Pfister, Marcus, 51
Pigs, 49
Pinky Dinky Doo, 67
Pinocchio, 13–14, 131–32
Pixar, 172
Please Do Not Open This Book, 32
Pocahontas, 157
The Pokey Little Puppy, 18, 20
Polyanna, 166
Postcards from Buster, 62
post-modern kid books, 43–46
Potter, Beatrix, 27

The Power Rangers, 81
The Prince of Egypt, 175
The Princess Diaries, 169
Propeller One-Way Night Coach, 34
Pryor, Richard, 56
"Puff the Magic Dragon," 108–10
"Put a Smile on Your Face," 105

Q

"Queer Visitors from the Marvelous
  Land of Oz," 54
quiz answers, 189–93
quiz, Books, 28–29
quiz, Disney Princesses, 144–47
quiz, Music, 106–7
quiz, Sesame Test, 71–73

R

Race for Your Life, Charlie Brown,
  125
"The Rainbow Connection," 102–3
The Rainbow Fish, 51
Ratatouille, 172
Raye, Colin, 117
Reading Rainbow, 67–68
"Ready Set Don't Go," 117
Reiner, Carl, 35
The Remarkable Farkle McBride, 38
The Rescuers Down Under, 154–55
The Rescuers, 150–51
Return to Oz, 57, 167–68
Revenge of the Sith, 79
Rey, H. A., 19
Rimes, LeAnn, 34
The Road to Oz, 54
Robin Hood, 149
Robots, 52
"Rock-a-Bye Baby," 120
Rolie Polie Olie, 52

Ross, Diana, 56
The Royal Book of Oz, 55
The Royal Guardsmen, 123
*Rudolph the Rednosed Reindeer and
  the Island of the Misfit Toys*, 40
Rugrats in Paris, 38
Ruiz, Aristides, 31
Ryman, Geoff, 57

S

Sagwa, 68
Saludos Amigos, 134
The Santa Claus, 168
Schoolhouse Rock, 117–120
Schulz, Charles, 121, 125
Scieszka, Jon, 44
The Sea Fairies, 54
The Secret of NIMH, 174
Seinfeld, Jerry, 34
Sendak, Maurice, 24
Sesame Street, 32–33, 60–61, 71–73
*Sesame Street Presents: Follow That
  Bird*, 173
Seuss, Dr., 30–31, 35, 91–95
Seussical the Musical, 94, 182
The Seven Lady Godivas, 30–31
The Shaggy Dog, 165
"She'll Be Coming Around the
  Mountain," 120
"Shower the People," 105
Shrek, 38
Shrek the Third: The Junior Novel,
  48
Shriver, Maria, 33
Silverstein, Shel, 35
Simon and Garfunkle, 105
A Simple Wish, 173
The Sissy Duckling, 37
Sky High, 169

Sleeping Beauty, 140–41
Smith, Jada Pinkett, 35
Smith, Will, 35
Smollin, Michael, 32
Snoopy Come Home, 124
Snoopy!!!: The Musical, 124
Snow White and the Seven Dwarves, 130–31
Snow, Jack, 55
The Snowy Day, 49–50
"Somewhere Over the Rainbow," 103–4
Song of the South, 171
Sorry, 184
The Sound of Music, 182
Space Jam, 170
Spiderman, 80
Spiegelman, Art, 121
Spirited Away, 175
Springsteen, Bruce, 101
Star Wars, 79
Stellaluna, 50
Stiles, Norman, 32
The Stinky Cheese Man and Other Fairly Stupid Tales, 45
Stone, Jon, 32
Superman, 79–80
The Swan Princess, 174
The Sword in the Stone, 142–43

T
"Take Me Out to the Ballgame," 120
The Tale of Peter Rabbit, 27
Tan, Amy, 29
Tartaglia, John, 65
Tarzan, 160
Taylor, James, 105
Teammates, 34
"Teddy Bear's Picnic," 100

Teletubbies, 68–69, 74
theater, 180–82
They Might Be Giants, 103
Thomas and the Magic Railroad, 173
Thompson, Ruth Plumly, 55
The Three Caballeros, 134–35
"Three is a Magic Number," 101, 117–20
Tin Man, 57
"The Tin Man," 105
Toby Tyler, or Ten Weeks with a Circus, 166
Today I Feel Silly and Other Moods That Make My Day, 39–40
Tomlin, Lily, 89
Toy Story, 172
Toy Story 2, 172
Travolta, John, 34
The Treasure Hunt, 39
Treasure Planet, 162–63
Trouble, 184
Trout Fishing in America, 99
The True Story of the Three Little Pigs, 44–45
Turner, Kathleen, 173
The 2000 Year Old Man Goes to School, 35
20,000 Leagues Under the Sea, 165

U
Updike, John, 29
The Upside Down Show, 69

V
Valenti, Jack, 129
Van Allsburg, Chris, 28
Vaughn, Stevie Ray, 104
Veggie Tales, 82

The Velveteen Rabbit, 16
The Very Hungry Caterpillar, 21
Voight, Jon, 173

W

Walken, Christopher, 173
"Walking on Sunshine," 105
Wallace and Gromit: The Curse of
    the Were-Rabbit, 177
Walter the Farting Dog, 50
Was, 57
"We're Gonna Be Friends," 102
Wells, Rosemary, 66
When Frank Was Four, 50
When I Was Little, 40
Where Do Balloons Go?, 40
Where the Wild Things Are, 24–26
Where's Waldo?, 41
The White Stripes, 102
Who Framed Roger Rabbit?, 171
"Who's Afraid of the Big Bad Wolf,"
    104
Who's Who in Oz, 56
Whoopi's Big Book of Manners, 35
Wicked, 57
The Wiggles, 110–15
The Wiggles World, 86
Wilco, 103
Williams, Margery, 16
Williams, Vanessa, 85–86
Willy Wonka and the Chocolate
    Factory, 176
The Wiz, 56, 173, 182
The Wizard of Oz, 55–56
The Woggle-Bug, 54
Wonder Pets, 69
The Wonderful Wizard of Oz, 52–57
The World's Greatest Athlete, 167
Worth, Bonnie, 31

Would You Like to Play Hide & Seek
    in This Book With Lovable, Furry
    Old Grover?, 32
The Wubbulous World of D. Seuss, 94
"Wynken and Blynken and Nod,"
    100–101

X

The X-Men, 80–81

Y

Yarrow, Peter, 109–10
A Year with Frog and Toad, 29
"Yellow Submarine," 105
Yertle the Turtle, 92
Yo Gabba Gabba, 70
You're a Good Man, Charlie Brown,
    123, 125

Z

Zathura, 28
Zoboomafoo, 70
Zoom, 88–89

About the Authors

Lou Harry, who is also co-author of *The High-Impact Infidelity Diet: a novel, The Complete Excuses Handbook,* and many other books, used to dream of traveling to Living Island, where H.R. Pufnstuf was mayor and the biggest threat was Witchipoo. Instead, he lives in Indianapolis with his wife and four kids and serves as arts and entertainment editor for the *Indianapolis Business Journal.* Visit him at myspace.com/louharry. Dress casual.

Todd Tobias is the co-author of *The Entourage Handbook* and *Put the Moose on the Table,* and there's a whole closet full of magazine articles he authored all by himself. If Barbra Walters were to ask "If he were a tree, what kind would he be?" he'd say "Shel Silverstein's *Giving Tree.*" He's quite certain this response would endear him to the audience. Or, at the very least, to his wife and two children.

About Cider Mill Press
Book Publishers

Good ideas ripen with time. From seed to harvest, Cider Mill Press strives to bring fine reading, information, and entertainment together between the covers of its creatively crafted books. Our Cider Mill bears fruit twice a year, publishing a new crop of titles each spring and fall.

Where Good Books are
Ready for Press

Visit us on the Web at
www.cidermillpress.com
or write to us at
12 Port Farm Road
Kennebunkport, Maine 04046